BELIEVE I TESTIFY

A collection of testimonies of answered prayers that will

increase your faith in God

Dedication

This book is dedicated to my three sons, Darnell, Anthony and Andre~, who has brought me so much joy, happiness and laughter. They taught me how to be a mother and appreciate God for giving me them. There is nothing like raising three sons. Also, to my grandson, Jewel, that I often call my "favorite grandson", which he always replied, "your only grandson". Because after I told him that I had written a book, he would periodically ask me when was I going to publish my book.

But most of all I would like to thank my Father God for giving His only begotten son for my salvation.

Without Him I would not be able to write this book.

Introduction

We used to sing this song in church and they probably still do, in some churches called *"Believe I Testify While I Have A Chance, I May Not Have A Chance Anymore"*. And it would prompt the people to stand up and give their testimony. We would hear some of the most awesome and inspirational testimonies and you would be surprised who testified about what God had done for them. I have heard people say "well this is a small testimony but I want to share what God has done". I never think of any testimony of what God has done as small. I knew what they meant but never-the-less, nothing God has done in the way of a blessing is small. I have a lot of wonderful testimonies that I want to share because God has been so good to me. Oh yes in these 56 plus years of being saved, I have gone through a number of trials, tribulations, challenges and tests of faith.

I've cried a lot of tears, had a lot of fears, lost loved ones and things, but in the midst of all of that, I held on to God. I had my testimonies, and my experiences from the past, that aided me in holding on. I want you, the reader, to be blessed from reading my testimonies, so you can see and know someone who have lived to experience the blessings of God. These testimonies are not in chronological order but in the order that God has given me to write them. So, prepare yourself to a few hours of reading my testimonies that comes from my heart.

I have enjoyed writing every word of this book, because I love sharing the things that God has done for me. I want the readers to know that God blesses and answers us in different ways and all areas. With God nothing is impossible or nothing is too small. We just have to learn to trust God at His Word, knowing that He is a kind, loving and mindful God. A God that takes care of His own. A God that keeps His promises and a God that will mold and make you to be what He wants you to be, if you let Him. He is a gentle God that does not force Himself upon you, but will show you how to get close to Him, welcoming you with open arms.

So, sit back and relax and I hope you will be blessed by the awesome testimonies, I have been willing to share, in this book.

About The Author

Sylvia is an ordained Minister and Teacher of the Word Of God. She authored and created a monthly newsletter, entitled S.U.A.R.T., Sisters United and Reunite Two Thousand for 17 years. The title had to be changed to S.U.A.R.T. And M.O.G.U.N. (Men of God United) because over a period of time, her newsletter was in demand by men, as well. She was married to her childhood sweetheart for 25 years who was instrumental in leading her to Christ. He is the father of her threes, as well as her lover, her friend and was one of her biggest fans. May he rest in peace.

She has had the privilege to be featured as an author in two compilations. "40 Days and 40 Nights" and "10 Answers That Changed My Life". As well as being featured in a short story in the inspirational magazine "Spirit Led Woman". Although it took her a while to get this book published, she never gave up nor lost her dream. She sees in her future other books she desires to write and have a greater determination like never before.

She lives in California and her hobbies consists of making jewelry, photography, collecting recipes and trying them. But she is an avid collector of fragrances which she thoroughly enjoys. Her prayer is that your faith grows while reading this book.

TABLE OF CONTENTS

Dedications from the Authors

Introduction

About the Author

Knowing My /Right From My Left

I learned how to drive in school, in my teens, but never had a car to drive until I was about 22 and married. Before taking the test, my girlfriend would take me out to drive so I could polish up on my driving. So, one day I went to the DMV to get my license. I get in my car with the instructor and we take off. While driving, he said "go to the next corner and make a right". I went to the next corner and made a left. He said "that was a good left but I wanted you to make a right". I apologized. Then I drive a little further and he said "make a left at the next corner". I drove to the corner and made a right. Well I guess he had enough, so he finally said "let's go back to the DMV". After we got there, he made some check marks and wrote on his pad. Then he said "show me your right hand", I did then he said "show me your left hand", and I did. He then said "I just wanted to make sure you knew your left from your right. Congratulations you passed your test". I was about to jump out of the car when he said "get your keys". I was just a nervous wreck taking that test and even with those mistakes, God gave me favor with the DMV. Thank You Lord.

Judge Not!

Years later I needed to renew my license by taking the written test. I hate to take these DMV tests. For some reason there is a "special" fear that comes over me when it comes to the DMV test, all other tests don't bring about this type of fear, but the DMV does. The questionnaire had 30 multiple choice questions,15 on each side. If you missed more than six you failed and had to take the test over, either on the same day or come back another time. Well after taking the test and standing in line, there were several clerks who would check your test. Looking at the different clerks I already said to myself, "I hope I don't get her", of course I was wrong by judging this person I didn't even know. And what difference would it make, because if I passed, I would be OK no matter who checked the test. Well guess what? I got her. She began to check my test. She started checking off the ones that was wrong on the first side. When she got to the bottom, she had already checked off five wrong answers. She looked at me and said, "Oh Sylvia", which mean, if there is five wrong on the first side, the chances are there are more than one on the other side. When she turned my sheet over there were more wrong, remember I said I hate these tests. She checked off at least three more. So that means I failed. She just balled up my paper and said "step into the half circles to take your picture for your license". Favor at the DMV again. How wrong was I to size her up and judge her? She was my blessing. The Word of God tells us not to judge and of course I repented and thanked God. *Matthews 7:13*

Favorite Color

If you knew me you would know that I love the color yellow. It is my favorite color to wear. It is such a happy carefree color that makes my heart smile. Every year in February and March I make sure I buy my yellow Daffodils and watch them bloom. I have even planted them and watch them come up, like clockwork in the early part of the year. Thank You Lord for creating that color. A lot of times it is the hardest color to find and often times not trendy. So, when I do find something in the color yellow, I take good care of it because I never know when I will find that color anytime soon.

One day, after work I was going to go to one of my favorite department stores, just to window shop and possibly to find something to buy. Just a few blocks before the store, right on the corner where I was about to make my left turn, there was a lady with her toddler, in a shopping cart, panhandling. I do give to people; I see on the streets in need because I feel for them. While approaching them, the Lord said "give them $5.00". I said "$5.00?" normally I will hand them a couple of dollars or three but not $5.00, but I obeyed. When I got to the store, as soon as I opened the door, I was hit with a display of the brightest yellow tee shirts I ever seen. I smiled and went over a purchased one. I was so happy to get my yellow shirt. I knew it was the Lord's doing. The scripture says "when you give to the poor, you lend to the Lord"

Proverbs 19:17 and you know when the Lord pays you back, He gives you more than you gave. Amen.

Going Home From Work

I was on my way home from work, driving down this road that was pretty dangerous. The city has since then, improved it tremendously. At that time, it was only two lanes and I was driving in the fast lane. I heard the Lord say "roll down your window". That struck me kind of strange, but I obeyed. As soon as I rolled down my window, I could hear my front tire flapping. I pulled over to the middle island that was covered with dirt. I got out and discovered I had had a blow-out that I didn't feel or hear. So, I pulled out my triple AAA sign and stood at the end of my car so I could hold it up, facing the oncoming traffic. Cell phones were invented but were very uncommon at that time to own by the general public.

While facing the traffic, I heard a voice behind me. A gentleman had pulled over in front of my car and I didn't even hear him, due to the noise of the moving traffic. He said, "I can change your tire but I don't have a jack". I didn't know if I had one but I knew I had a spare. So as soon as I opened my trunk, this young lady, with her small child, pulled up and said, "I can't change a tire but I have a jack". Yea I know you find that hard to believe, but it's true. He took my spare out and changed my tire. The young lady got in her car and drove off waving good-bye. I tried to offer the man some money and he strongly refused. He said he just wanted to help. I lost about 15 minutes of my time of getting home. Driving home and praising God and in total disbelief of what just happened. I didn't disbelieve God at all, but everything happened so quick. I mean God made this an open and shut case within 15 minutes, plus later I found out I did have a jack. Bless Him!

Going To Work

I had to be at work at 6:00 AM, so I had to travel in the dark. As I was on my way to work, same car, same road just a couple of years later, I got a flat. A man pulled up in front of me, got out of his car and said "I can't change your tire but you can use my cell phone, (now cell phones are a little more common), to call triple AAA". So, I called them and handed him back his phone. He handed it back to me and said "here I know you need to call your job and let them know you will be late", which I did. I thanked him and he got back in his car and drove off. Shortly after that the sun started to come up and triple AAA arrived and changed my tire. Now before you think I have bad tires, not to the contrary, these are just everyday things that happens to every one of us. And when you have God in your life, protecting you, He shows you what He does and how He does it. Also, needless to say I got me a cell phone after that.

God Will Direct You

Proverbs 3:6 says, "Acknowledge the Lord in all thy ways, and He will direct thy path." This is one of those scriptures we know and often quote but seldom practice. When we do practice it, it is when we are facing something big and really need directions. Then we pray, fast, and meditate on how to handle a situation, but God really wants us to acknowledge Him in all our ways. Nothing is petty or too small to talk to Him about. If we put this into practice more, we will often make our lives a whole lot easier. One day, after work, I had to go to three different places before going home. I needed to go to the post office, the grocery store and the bank. Depending on the last place I went to would determine which way I would go home. I had two different routes to go home and one would not get me home any faster than the other. Plus, I didn't need to go to the bank first because I was making a deposit. So, as I sat in my car, I said "Lord where should I go first and last?" He said "go to the grocery store first, then the bank and then go across the street to the post office, and go home the San Pablo Dam Road way". So, I said "OK". I did just that.

Well after leaving the bank and driving across the street to the post office, when I got out of my car, on this very windy day, I could see some balled up money blowing towards me. I could not believe my eyes because I could see a $20.00 dollar bill in this cash ball. I just reached down and picked it up. It was a $20.00 dollar bill and a $10.00 dollar bill. The parking lot was almost empty in this normally full lot. I went into the post office to see if someone was looking for money, they had lost, but it was only one senior person in there and he had just walked in right before I did and the money had started blowing towards me a long way behind him. My heart was happy that I had obeyed and put that scripture into practice that day. One might think that that was a silly question to ask God, but it wasn't.

Again, He said for us to acknowledge Him in all our ways and He will direct our paths. Amen.

Airplane Crash

While coming home from work, all of a sudden, I saw a small plane, that was really close, descending really fast and it was turned on its side. There were others on the highway, and we just looked at each other with our mouths open, in total disbelief knowing that this plane was going to crash. We all stopped, and got out of our cars to look down over the overpass where the plane had landed. One of the wings was right there on the highway and on fire and as we looked down where the plane had landed, there was a sudden explosion with a large cloud of black smoke. We could not believe our eyes. Sad to say, it was obvious that the pilot died. No one on the highway was hurt, thank God, and had I been about 20 seconds earlier more than likely the plane wing would have hit my car and maybe others. All I could do when I got home was thank God.

I love testimony service because you get a chance to hear the testimonies of other people who won the victory by trusting God or waiting on God. You get a chance to hear that others have went through the same things that you are going through and how they dealt with their trial through prayer and belief. You get a chance to share how you dealt with adversities which ends up being a help to others. We are overcomers by the words of our testimonies and we help others to become overcomers. *Revelations 12:11*

The One Thousand Dollar Gift

After my husband and I separated, I no longer had his help in maintaining my fairly new car. So, I kept driving it not knowing I needed to periodically get the oil changed. It was my only way to get back and forth to work and to my second job as a Nail Technician. So, one day the engine was blown, completely destroyed. I was not able to get it fixed and desperately needed to get to work and to get to the nail salon. Where I lived, at the time, was several blocks from the main street to catch the bus. So, I had to get up early and walk quite a way, in the dark in order to catch the bus. I was late to work a lot of times, not overly, but late. I had to hustle to get home before dark and on Thursday, Friday and Saturdays I had a hard time getting to the nail salon, which I needed to get to because I had a decent clientele and the money, I made from my nail business was a tremendous help. I would get to the shop, which was in the opposite direction from where I lived. Then hustle a ride home, and if I caught the bus coming home from the shop, I would have one of my sons meet me at the bus stop because it would be nighttime when I got home.

I needed to keep my nail business going even though it was a task to get there, because the money was pretty good. I would make around $200.00 a day which of course I needed because of my current situation, plus my sons all had incomes and they helped a great deal to keep food in the house and a roof over our heads. I bless God for that. There were times a co-worker would be going in my direction but not as far but she would always tell me when she was going my way and would take me all the way home. She said she understood what I was going through and even though I did not broadcast to everyone what I was going through, I did share my problems with a few and everyone I confided in were so helpful to me. She would insist on taking me all the way home and would never want any money for gas. And even though she had no children she still understood my dilemma. That right there is something to bless God for because some people are not sensitive to other people's problems.

During that time my supervisor never said a word about me getting to work late and leaving early, on those days I had a ride. Not one word. On one Saturday I just could not get a ride to the nail salon. Sometimes my sister would take me and bring me back home and she lived miles from where I lived. But on this particular day, I had no ride. So, I just laid on my bed, after cleaning my house to just meditate and think and imagine the money I was missing. Shortly, my telephone rang, and it was the owner of the beauty shop, where I rented space. She asked me what was I doing and I told her I was laying on top of my bed, doing nothing. She said "get up you need a friend!". She began to tell me how; at the time of her divorce she was angry and treated her friends mean but they understood and stood by her anyway. She said she would be that friend to me. Now keep in mind I had only met her the year before so I had not known her that long, and I had met her through a friend of ours who recommended that I call her for a spot in her shop. She said her divorce was almost settled, from her husband who was a professional ball player and as soon as she got her money, she was going to give me $1,000.00, which would help me get my car fixed. In about two weeks after that she gave me the money.

I had just talked to a childhood friend I hadn't seen in about 25 years and he told me about a mechanic around the corner from where he lived who could possibly help. I called the mechanic and told him the problem with my car. I had the car towed to his shop and he discovered that the engine was destroyed from the build-up of thick oil, from not having the oil changed, so I needed a new engine. By this time three or four months had passed and I was still making payments on the car. Can you imagine the frustration of everyday looking at your disabled car that you are making payments on? I didn't want to stop making payments and ruin my credit, plus I found out my husband had just quit making insurance payments, just imagine. After my car was at the repair shop for about two weeks, the mechanic called to tell me he had just found a car, that had been in an accident, that totaled it out but the engine was perfect, a year younger than my car, and had less mileage, that would fit and would cost $1,600.00 to fix. I said "go for it". I gave him the $1,000.00 and after two weeks, after I finished paying him, he released my car. I was able thank God to get back on the road and that car lasted another 10 more years after that. Also, I forgot to mention that the location where the engine blew was about 30 miles from my house. I didn't have the coverage or money to pay to have it towed to my house. But a friend of mine had a friend who worked for a towing company, who was willing to tow my car home, after hours, for $20.00. Won't He do it?

$.99 Cents Eyeglasses

As we get older, a number of us need to wear readers, you probably have on a pair, right now while reading this book. After losing, breaking and misplacing readers someone told me to go to the .99 cent store to get extra pairs. So, I did and I kept extra pair at work, in the car, in my purse, by my bedside and the family room. They would break, get lost or misplaced like all glasses do so I would periodically visit the .99 cent store for extra pairs. I certainly am not against the .99 cent store but I don't frequent them that often and when I do, I am reminded of their awesome bargains. One day I went to our local. 99 cents store I had never been in and while looking around I remembered to go check out the readers. While looking this man came from "nowhere" and plopped this box of readers in my cart and said "you might find some good ones in here". The box was full of Foster Grants retailing up to $16.00 a pair. I picked out about seven pair and I even called my friend and asked her what power, of glasses she used. I thought, hey this is a cool .99 cent store. I have been in that store several times since and have never found any Foster Grants since. I am so glad I took advantage of that blessing. I was at the right place at the right time.

Going The Extra Mile

After working as an overseas operator for about six years I got a promotion to word processing better known as the typing pool. I loved that job especially since I love writing. The typing jobs would be inhouse documents the employees needed typed. That consisted of forms and/or written narratives or letters. While in that job I got promoted to lead clerk. So, I was no longer a typist but I would assign the jobs, to the typists, keep track of its progress, proof read it to make sure there were no errors, call the in-house "customer" to let them know that their documents were ready for pick-up. After being lead clerk for about two years I was ready for another promotion and another change. Promotions were all over the place but someone with higher seniority would beat me out. So, I just waited until another job would come up.

One day this upper management person came in with a typing job. I logged the job in and gave him a date and the time the job would be ready. I gave it to one of the typists. The due date came and the manager came in to pick up his work which was overdue but was not ready. He was disappointed and so was I. I spoke to the typist and told them to speed up doing the job. A couple of days went by and the job still wasn't done. My job as the lead clerk was to take in the job, log it in, give the customer the receipt with the turn-around time, proof it and call to let them know their job was ready. It was my supervisor's job to put the pressure on the typist. So, after the second time the job wasn't ready, I told the manager that I would personally type up his job right away and I called him and told him it was ready for pickup. He was pleasantly surprised. He then told my supervisor that he had a higher position that had come available and that he wanted me to fill the position. I got the job and the promotion, and I didn't have to go through all the hoops and requirements to get it.

Job Relocation

After several years of being in my current job, the company decided to open up a new office in a faraway unincorporated location. This means several hundred of us were going to have to go along with the company's move. Most of us were very unhappy about this and could do nothing about it. We just had to roll with the punches. Most of us hated the ides of this new move, it was just so inconvenient. We first started out in van pools, then carpools because some employees started to relocate by moving closer to the work area. Soon it got down to two people carpooling, then just me driving by myself. Sometimes I would cry on my way to work which was an hour away. I would be miserable going to work. A couple of times my car broke down and that was no fun.

This went on for about three or four years. There were locations closer to home and also located where I could take public transportation, but they were very hard to get a job there because positions very seldom came up. But I kept trying and making phone calls and speaking to my contacts every now and then. My supervisor knew how bad I wanted to transfer from Pleasanton to Oakland and he did all he could, but to no avail. He even talked to the supervisors in Oakland and introduced me to people I already knew telling them I was qualified. I even spent one day on a trial basis just for them to test me out. It's just that jobs were as rare as hen's teeth in Oakland.

My supervisor applied for an upper management position for himself because he was ready to move on as well. A few weeks later he got the offer for his promotion. Now this meant a lot more money for him. It didn't mean a money increase for me to go to Oakland it just means salvation for my sanity and wellbeing. He told the person who offered him his promotion he would only take the job if they found a job for me in Oakland, shortly and I mean shortly after that I got the job, relocated and once again become a happy camper. God can and will step into your situation to make your life better and it is not always about money.

Parking Lot Soap

On Saturday's when I was still working, I would do my shopping. Mainly for groceries and household needs. So that would possibly mean I went to several stores and places of business. I always make a list for each store and would go from store to store. I was in my favorite drug store just walking around after I had gotten my items on my list and I remembered I needed some detergent, so as I was turning to go to the home cleaning isle, the Lord said plainly "don't get your detergent here you are going to the grocery store, get it there". I literally turned in my tracks and said "yes OK Lord'. I checked out and went to the grocery store. As soon as I parked my car and got out, right there in the parking lot was the largest box of Surf detergent I had ever seen. Now Surf is not cheap and not the detergent I was going to buy at the other store because they didn't carry it. I promptly put the detergent in my car. When I got inside the store, I went over to the detergent to see what the value of such a large box was, there was not one box of Surf that size in the store and I looked carefully. That confirmed that I knew I heard what the Lord said.

Now for you sceptics who thought I took someone else's detergent, first of all God does not have to take from someone else to bless someone else. I believe He has but also, I knew that that box of Surf was placed there, by God, for me because He told me what to do and I heard Him clearly. God can and will bless you anyway He chooses. That box of Surf lasted me for the longest time and I kept wondering when was it going to run out. Thank You Lord for saving me money, once again. And just as a side note, a few years after that, as I passed the hall bathroom, one day, I got this wonderful smell of soap after my son had taken his shower. I said to him, "wow that is some great smelling soap you showered in". He said, "oh that was some Ivory soap, I found an eight-pack brick of it in the parking lot". Go figure. Are we on to something?

Bank Forgiveness

Before I married my second ex-husband, I had overdraft protection with my bank. They offered so I signed up for it, but in the past, I was never interested in being in that program I have always made it a practice to have the money in the bank for any checks I wrote. I've tried to be a good steward in all that I do. If I wrote a check to anyone you never heard from my mouth "go cash this check right away". That's just not me. Plus, I learned that if they covered a check you were short on, not only was there a fee but also a charge of $5.00 a day for each day until you took care of it. After being married a few months he found out I had $1,000.00 check overdraft protection. He asked me what did that mean and reluctantly I told him. He seemed happy about that and later I found out why, (one reason he is an Ex). I'm sure I had had this coverage for several years before I met him and never used it. I was only married to him for 17 months because he had begun to start doing things that made me realize I had made a mistake and this is not who I wanted to be with nor how I wanted to live. Yes, there were subtle signs, but I thought they were minor and he got progressively worse as time went on. My responsibility was to pay the bills and his was to pay the rent. At first it worked, until he found out about the plan I had with the bank. He began to be short on the rent and that made the plan kick in and I wasn't about to cover him nor let him know about my personal savings I had before I married him.

When my first marriage came to an end I was left in a bad financial state and I wasn't going to allow this to happen to me again. Thank God there are some things that need to happen just once for you to learn. So, he was short again and this was very close to our marriage coming to an end. I hated that this had happened but there was nothing I could do about owing the bank. So, I was stuck and the marriage was over. I felt bad that I owed the bank this money and had ruined my credit. I knew I had to talk to the bank about settling this plus I wanted no communication with my Ex., as I was so glad that that marriage was over. I always took pride in my good credit.

So, after I got settled, I went to the bank and asked to see someone in management. I explained to him my situation and I told him that I had all intentions of paying them back. I was apologetic and sincere in my explanation He got up from his desk and said let me get your file. He came back and told me he spoke to another manager, after showing him my file and they agreed that I could make payments of my choice, take the time I needed and also, they discovered I had $49.00 in my closed account and he gave me that money. Now who does that? Thank God for being so thoughtful and so understanding and most of all so loving. The most prayerful of us, the strongest of us and the most read up of us can and do make mistakes. That's why when we do make mistakes we get back up, ask for forgiveness and guidance and also ask for more sensitivity to the guidance of the Holy Spirit. Don't forget the cross, why the cross and what happened at the cross. God is forgiving and so should we be forgiving. Because being forgiving sets us free.

Believe I Testify

I have heard how saints of God get mistreated and disrespected by others, by their boss, co-workers, clerks and other people they come in contact with. In this walk persecution does come but not all the time, from everyone. We as children of God have to be careful and watch how we act, respond and approach people. We who are Godly are to be Godly with everyone not just other Christians. We are under a magnifying glass, and we are under other people's telescopes. We must practice to be like Jesus in every area of our lives. We have the ability to win souls for Christ by our actions. Scripture says, "with loving kindness have I drawn thee". When you approach in love and in kindness you will find you will be treated better by others, whether they are believers or not, *Jeremiah 31:3.*

Surprise Promotion

When you have worked as long as I have you have many encounters with co-workers, supervisors, upper managers and the general public I have worked for one company for over 30 years, retired from that job and then worked another 10 years for another organization. Not to mention all the other short timed jobs I have had, so I have a lot of experience of dealing with people Another blessing that stands out is when I started working for a large communications company. I was an overseas operator and I loved that job. Mainly because it was a new experience for me and I loved the many shifts I had to choose from that fit right into my personal needs for my children and husband. I held that position for six years and at that time, had no desire to change because of the ideal shifts that were available. Well time came for the office to close down and move to Colorado and most of us did not want to move from the Oakland Bay Area. So, the next alternative was to locate to San Francisco which I loved anyway. This transfer was causing us to promote from operator to clerk and in order to do that we had to pass a typing test. Originally under normal circumstances you would have to go to San Francisco and take the test there but since it was so many of us, the supervisor that gave you the test and determined if you were qualified, came to Oakland on her own time and brought typewriters for us to practice on in our own time. I took advantage of this, especially since I hadn't typed in years. So, every now and then the supervisor would give us a trial typing test so we could see how it would be when it was time to take the real test. So, she gave me a trial to practice and I would do ok, but still needed more practice time. So, then she gave me another practice test and when I took it, she said "OK you're ready. As a matter of fact, I will use this as your real test. You passed, you qualify and I have the perfect job for you". I was placed in the typing pool, better known as the Word Processing Center, which helped start my ability to edit. He will do it every time!

Another Surprise Promotion?

After I retired from AT&T I rested for a while then I started working at my favorite drug store. I have always enjoyed working in sales and retail and the store was less than five minutes away from my house, an ideal situation, I thought. I filled out my application, I believe on a Friday and on Sunday when I came home from church there was a voice mail telling me I was hired. Hired on a Sunday, by voice mail, how interesting. I just wanted to work part time to supplement my pension. Well they gave me a little more than part time hours and that was ok, because the hourly wage was small so this gave me more money. They started giving me back-to-back shift, which I didn't like. I didn't like working late then coming in early the next day.

Plus, there was this one manager no one really cared for. We hated when she was in charge. She was mean, hardly smiled, acted as if she was mad when you needed her and just had this hard taskmaster mentality. So, I told the head manager I wanted to quit because of the back-to-back shifts and because of this particular manager. She told me no I could not quit. What? She said I was too good of an employee to quit. So, she said she would make changes for me. Not give me so many back-to-backs and make sure my hours of work would be scheduled where I would have to work mostly when this manager was off. This worked for a while but soon I quit one day when the head

37

manager was off so I would not have to face her because she was such a nice person.

So, I was off from work again for a few more months. I signed up with this temp agency that was known for placing you with jobs in a short time after passing their test. After taking the test and passing, she said I passed a particular part of the test that most people fail. I got placed on a few one-day jobs that paid very well but I needed a long-term assignment. They called me one day and said they had a job that didn't pay what I wanted but it was a long-term assignment. I went ahead and accepted it because it was time for me to get back to work, somewhere.

I caught on quick with this job at social services and I loved the job. After about a week the supervisor went and got an application and told me to fill it out because she wanted me to become permanent. But with social services you have to wait until the job is offered and they interview at least six people for that job, plus you have to wait until they are testing for jobs. So, after about four months we heard that they would be testing in two months. I started asking questions as to how this works. So first I had to pass a typing test, then a multiple-choice test, then wait hopefully for an interview. There was this person who had been a temp for about six years but could never pass the test. She was well known and well liked because when one unit no longer needed her another unit would grab her up. She befriended me and began to educate me on the possible questions that was on the test. She even bought expensive books on how to pass the county tests and would give them to me. I felt uncomfortable taking her books but she insisted and God let me know this was His favor working for me. After using her books, I would return them not feeling like I learned anything because to me the questions were hard and how do you know which questions would be on your test. It was set up almost like the DMV test.

The time came and I took the test. The room was full of people and they were testing hundreds of people because they had a ton of positions that would soon be opening. I was the second one finished and I wondered did I miss something because the test seemed easier than I thought. Now here's the scary part. Even though I was a temp and they needed to fill the position that I was in did not mean I would get that particular job, but I didn't know that. I thought I would be offered the job I was in, because after I passed the test I started getting offers for interviews for other jobs. And I would pass the interview, get a phone call offering me the job and I would turn them down. One interview I went on was for a clerical position for the district attorney's office. They told me "don't call us we'll call you in a few weeks". They called me the next day offering me the position and I turned them down. I shared this with my co-workers and they yelled at me and said "no Sylvia don't turn down any offers, it doesn't go like that". If you turn down offers your name goes on a list to never be called again. I was thinking have I messed myself up?

A few days later my supervisor whispered in my ear that the division manager wanted me for the position I was in but still I had to go through the process. I told her I was turning down offers and she said she would set up the interview to go through the motions so I can be offered the job. Needless to say, I got my job. The funny thing about the interview is the three supervisors who were in on the interview all had this look on their faces as if to say "you know and we know the end results". After about an hour my supervisor called me in her office and offered me the job I stayed in that position, by choice for about six years then I moved on to another position, then retired after 10 years. Yes, you read correctly, I retired again.

Just a tidbit of advice, I learned when you work for social services you can move up quickly because they have a lot of opportunity, at least at the time I was there. I even promoted to social worker but after assessment of my age I gave that position up while in training and returned to my clerical position. Had I been younger I would have kept that position, but I gave that up for someone else to have that opportunity, even though I was passing and doing well while in training. God is so good, isn't He? What God has for you He sees that you get it and I was so blessed to be able to return to my last position.

The Sympathetic Supervisor

In one's lifetime many things happen. Some things could have been avoided and other things just cannot. A child falling and bumping their heads, a car accident or even a bill collector calling. All these things happen in life. Some things that happens are expected or surprises When I would think about living without my mother, the only parent I knew, I would imagine myself being devastated and I would abandon the thought. While at work, one day, I got that dreaded call that my mother was just rushed to the hospital after being worked on by the paramedics. Worked on what does that mean? But I knew what it meant. By the time I got to the hospital she had passed on. Through the strength of God, I was able to function and do whatever I needed to do. And shortly after her burial I was able to thank God for not letting her suffer. I was stronger than I thought I would be all because of God.

My job allowed up to seven days off for death of a parent. That is where I had the most difficulty. I was not ready to return to work after seven days. I called my supervisor and talked to her and she said take all the time you need, don't worry about it. I believe I took about two weeks. My pay was not cut and I

got paid in full for the entire time I was off, which was a blessing. They don't usually do that. It is just a wonderful thing to be in the favor of

God. Of course, I miss my mother, but I thank God that I was able to introduce her to Christ in the fullness. She always believed but after I got saved, she saw the changes in my life and was able to really understand more about salvation.

Favor From Former Supervisor

The first long term job I had, I put in nearly 31 years. I never knew when I would retire especially since I didn't have the age requirement that avoided me paying high taxes since I had started so young, AT&T started making offers in the form of package deals for retirement. At first, offers were not made to my level then finally they started making us the offer. It was a pretty decent offer, but I was a little skeptical. And everyone was saying "oh they will make another offer and it would probably be better". But they didn't know that. No one knew, but upper management. So, I decided to wait and see if another offer would be made to us. The deadline date was set and it came and went. So, we spent the next six weeks celebrating and congratulating those who would be leaving soon, those who took the package deal. The retirement offer included a lump sum of money, five years added to your age, which they called a sweetener, so you wouldn't be taxed so highly and your pension in a lump sum if you wanted it in a lump sum or monthly pension payments. Nice deal huh?

This offer was made in early January and the deadline date was the last day in January to make your decision and your last day would be the last day in March. The first Sunday in March I was in church and we were singing and clapping our hands, praising God and having a good time. All of sudden I thought about work and that dreaded commute and that horrible position I held, that I just despised. I made up my mind, that I got to retire, I've had enough. I knew I had missed the deadline date, but I had a plan because I knew this was God's plan.

When I got to work, I went to my desk, logged on, put away my personal things and went upstairs to my former supervisor who had gotten a promotion to division manager. Plus, he was my favorite supervisor out of all of the supervisors I had had over the years and we had a good supervisor/subordinate relationship when I worked for him. During the time I reported to him I would ask him had he had lunch because he would work so hard and he would say "no" and ask me where was I going for lunch. I would either tell him where I was going or ask where he would like for me to go. When his wife got pregnant, I gave him the biggest surprise baby shower ever because for one reason, they had miscarried their first and he was just so nice to me. He was the best supervisor I had plus I loved his laid-back carefree attitude. I didn't feel he owed me I just knew we had had a good relationship and I knew he was the man.

He looked at me as I entered his office and said "Sly (my nickname), what are you doing here?" I said "I got to go, and I want the package deal". He said, "you know that the window is closed and it's too late". And I said "I know that's why I am here in your office. He said, "well let me see what I can do". I went back to my desk and began to work.

After about 45 minutes I looked up and he was at my desk and he said, "come Sly I have some important people on my phone upstairs that you need to talk to". When I stood up, I looked at my co-workers and my supervisor and they all had this shocked look on their faces. Because, first of all, when he showed up at someone's desk that meant they were fired or in big trouble. I said nothing I just followed him, leaving my co-workers with their mouths opened.

That cracks me up every time I think about this. When I got on the phone the person on the other end said "so you want to retire", and I said "yes", then he said "ok it's approved, congratulations". I was very happy and I got a little teary eyed because I knew I would miss everyone I had met and became close to over the years but it was time. When I came back to my desk, I told my supervisor what had just taken place. Now I will explain why I went over her head, first of all I follow God's leading. Second of all she was new at being a supervisor and she didn't know me that well and I knew she would have said to me what I already knew about the deadline and I don't believe she would have followed through in a timely manner nor go to the right people. I knew the leading of God and I followed it. My former supervisor and I had good history between us and I always tried to have a good relationship between me and my managers. They are not your enemies they are human just like we are and are some of the best people to build a good relationship with. It will someday pay off, because we do reap what we sow and often times we reap more than what you sowed.

Unexpected Refund

Sometimes when you are expecting money, a refund, a payment, or money owed to you from a friend, in the mail and you really need it, it's hard to wait. You go to the mailbox promptly every day until it arrives. When it does you are happy and glad that the wait is over. I had such a refund I was expecting and really needed it. The amount was $1,500.00 and a few days after I knew the money was due, I kept going down the street to my mailbox to see if it had arrived. Every day after work I would check the mailbox and this went on for about a week and a half until one day, when I got off work, I decided not to check because I was tired of being disappointed. I said to myself "I'll check tomorrow when I get off work". The next morning, I decided to check instead of waiting until the end of the day.

When I got the mail out, I could see that there were two checks, now you know I was happy. While driving I opened one check. It was for $440.00 and I got a little nervous because I wondered what the other check was for. I desperately needed at least the $1,500.00 I was expecting. But before I opened the next letter I stopped thinking about my needs and I began to praise God and I said, "Lord I thank You for the $440.00 I just received and whatever the other check is I will give you praise and I will give You the glory". I opened the other check and it was for $1,800.00, $740.00 more than I expected and of course I was happy, thank You Lord. Thank you for loving me the way that You do. And I could hear The Lord say to me, I could have had you open the larger check first, I just wanted your praise". This amount not only allowed me to take care of my responsibilities but also allowed me to do so shopping for myself and help someone else who was in need. Thank You Lord for some shopping money, because You know I love to shop.

I'll Send Her Instead

As far as I can remember I have always loved to write. Ideas would come in my head and I love to put it on paper, for personal reasons and to share with others. And when I got that job in Word Processing it helped me in my writing skills, especially in editing. When I read someone else's writing I can see and "feel" how to re-write their material without changing what they were trying to say. And whenever I made changes in someone's work, I always let them know this. I believe every one of us have more than one gift. I also believe each one of us is expert in at least one gift and gifted in many areas. And after finding out what they are we should do all we can to perfect that gift. Some people know just the right spices to put in a dish. They know the right colors to put an outfit together to make it pop. Or the right color to paint the interior of a house. They know how to organize your cabinet, your closet or your bill paying method to keep you on a budget that works for you. Some people can teach like no other, especially the Word of God. I love to sit under a strong Bible teacher that you can tell that they study in depth. You yourself know what you are good at. Perfect your gifts and work hard at being an expert at it.

Several years after leaving Word Processing and doing something entirely different, my supervisor was required to go to a proof-reading class. Yep, a proof-reading class. He wasn't happy about having to attend, because he had zero interest in attending, nor wanting to know how to proofread. So, he came up with an excuse and told them he would send me in his place. He had no knowledge of my past work history, he just picked me and told me he had submitted my name to go. I would have never signed up for that class but it was right up my alley and I was glad to go. And of course, that class helped me in my editing skills. You see me referring to writing, editing and being a word processor often because God will bless you where you are. He knows those gifts He has put in us and if we are in His way, He will make provisions for you to perfect them. Here's another one coming up.

One On One Writing Class

A few years after being with social services, a writing class was offered to help the social workers in their writing of their report and the class was offered to every level. The job I had at the time contained a lot of writing of reports but not as extensive as a social worker. I signed up as well because I was/am the publisher of an inspirational newsletter and thought I could get some points and ideas. This was an all day class and these classes are being taught by outside vendors and they are very costly. That's why it is mandatory to attend if you sign up because of the cost involved. When I got to the class early no one was there yet but the instructor, a very nice person I observed. After about 15 minutes no one else came to the class. The instructor said she was going to tell the division manager that there was only one person in the class and she wanted to know what to do. This also shows you how overwhelmed the social workers are with work, because they don't have time to attend needed classes. Anyway, she came back with the manager and the manager said, "well Sly I guess you will get personal training because no other social worker is available, and we have to pay the instructor regardless". You can't beat favor, you can't knock favor and no one can stop favor.

I told her that I was the author of a newsletter and that I was not a social worker and she said, "go get a copy of your newsletter and I will use that as my material to teach from". She was a Christian and she loved my newsletter, she asked to be placed on my mailing list and we spent the whole day together and she gave me a lot of insight on writing. Can't you just see why I wrote this book? I have a deluge of God's blessings and favor and open doors and closed doors against me in my history of life, living for God. And no matter how much He has blessed me I still end up with and open mouth when He moves in my favor. Because we are so undeserving of the things God does for us, but His mercy and grace and favor never stops. I have so much to praise Him for and trust me when you get to the end of this book, there are still tons of testimonies I have forgotten. I want you to see in this book how God works and what He does and how He does the things for us.

He may bring your blessings in your life in a different way but He keeps them coming if we serve Him, praise Him and most importantly live for Him. Sometimes I can just be quiet at home or in my car or just out and about and I began to think about all that He's has done. And I think about the promises He has told me about and I get overwhelmed with praise and tears. I mean we serve a mighty God and an awesome God. Nothing He does is small. Sometimes I hear people say "I have a small testimony of what God has done", and I cringe because I don't see His blessings as small. Now I know what they mean when they say that. Sometimes you can compare a $1,000.00 blessing to a $1.00 blessing, but a $1.00 blessing could be just what you needed to get a bus ticket home. It could be just what you need to put enough gas in your car to get home or just what you needed to buy that loaf of bread for your family. At that time that dollar was a huge blessing not a small one. Let's stop putting a size on God's blessings because whatever He does for us is huge.

I Gotta Leave This Town!

In 1989 I had been working in Oakland for four years after transferring from Pleasanton and I loved it because I was closer to home and no longer had that long awful commute and Oakland was only 20 minutes away from where I lived. And if I didn't drive, I could take Bart, our rapid transit. In October of that year we had the infamous Loma Prieta earthquake that did a lot of damage in the San Francisco Bay Area. Our building was damaged, but we were able to continue to work in the building. As time went on it was getting close to the time where we would be moving out so they could start the long repair process. A lot of us were split and some of my co-workers had to go as far as Atlanta on three weeks on, two weeks off system because of their duties. It was a mess and I felt sorry for those who had to do this because it took them away from their families. And as time went on the company began to offer enough money for them to relocate in Atlanta on a permanent basis, to buy homes, especially if they wanted to keep their job. Fortunately, I was not part of that group. But the only two places I had available for my relocation was Walnut Creek or back to that dreaded Pleasanton. We had no say, and we had no choice, we just knew that one day we would be approached, individually with the news of what location we were selected to go to. So, this also meant a new job function as well, same level, same salary, new function, doing what, we did not know. I was nervous, but I prayed. Being nervous is an emotion and it does not mean a lack of faith, but nervousness can come about during the unknown or when your fate lies in someone else's hands. In this kind of situation, the best thing to do is pray and tell the Lord what you want. Telling God does not mean He doesn't know, to the contrary, because He knows everything. He wants to hear it from you. Making your request known to God is what the Bible says to do. *Philippians 4:6, "Be careful for nothing, but in everything by prayer and supplication, with thanksgiving let your requests be made known unto God"*

As time went on some of my co-workers started getting the bad news that they were being relocated to Pleasanton and this put a bittersweet atmosphere in the office. Even some of my closest friends had to go there not to mention those who were forced to go to Atlanta. While sitting at my desk, one day, my supervisor approached me and whispered in my ear, "Monday after next you will be reporting to Walnut Creek". All I could do was sit there while my eyes welled up in tears and she saw my reaction and was glad for me. Walnut Creek was in the opposite direction from where I lived and was 20 minutes away and I could take the Bart if I wanted to plus the beauty of it all I was going to be reunited with some of my friends I used to work with in the past so I wasn't going to be working with strangers.

Your Apartment Is Ready

Romans 8:28 "And now we know that all things work together for good to them that love God, to them who are the called according to his purpose".

After going through a lot of trials, test and tribulations for years we should be able to look back and see everything that we went through was for our good. After being single for eight years from my first marriage, I married again. It was a very unpleasant marriage that lasted 17 months. Then we broke up because I left the marriage because he was abusive, and I was not going to live under no one's abuse. God did not put us here on this earth to tolerate abuse from anyone. That is one thing I don't understand how a person, man or woman feel they have to stay in an abusive relationship, like that is the best they can do, well not me. I found myself in a situation where I had to put all my furniture in storage and live with someone for about six weeks.

Downstairs from where I was staying was a two-bedroom apartment that was occupied and I never even gave it a thought of living there. I thought I would be where I was until the first of the year which was a couple months away and my 401K would be freed up and I could find a place of my own. Sometimes they would put a freeze on our 401K for whatever reason and we could not draw any money from it. Little did I know that the landlord was preparing the downstairs for me. Also, there was a large one bedroom house, he had built, right next door, by the way, that I knew nothing about and it was unoccupied. He really was a genius when it came to building homes. In fact, I don't remember saying two words to him at all but he had a plan, or should I say, God had a plan? Unbeknownst to me the landlord had his son, who lived downstairs, move into the one bedroom so he could get the downstairs ready for me.

One day after getting off from work, I was resting and my niece said, "Auntee, Elvyn wants you to come look at your place". What?", Elvyn? What place?" I thought out loud. I was half asleep and confused, I said "place, where?" And she said "downstairs. Then I entered into the cutest two-bedroom place you could imagine. It was newly painted, curtains were bright and clean, it had a large living room, wet bar, walk-in food pantry, washer and dryer hook-up, appliances and fully carpeted I was breathless. He told me the price and I told him I couldn't pay his asking price and told him what I could afford which was $150.00 less than he was asking. He never said, "are you crazy"?, he just kept saying, "look how nice it is, look how clean the curtains are", and he was right. The place was worth what he was asking but I wasn't ready to pay what he wanted. We went back and forth, and he settled for $25.00 over what I could pay. He never asked for a deposit nor first and last and he had to wait a few days for me to get the money, because all my money was tied up. Plus, I lived there for eight years and he never, I said never raised the rent. How about that!?

My furniture was in two storage places because I had a lot of furniture from moving from a four bedroom, completely furnished house. I decided to empty the smaller storage first because it had my two couches, two loveseats, living room furniture, TV, bedroom, CD's and my entertainment stuff.

Got to have my music. Then after getting settled I would move my stuff from the other storage facility.

My washer, dryer, dinette set and tables, other bedroom furniture, lamps, and clothes would come later.

The very next day after I moved my stuff from the first storage there was a flash flood in the area where it was located. I got a phone call from the storage people saying that they were sorry to inform me, but my furniture had been covered in four feet of water because my stuff was on the ground floor. I told them I had just moved out the day before. Now how close is that? That would be the last thing I needed was for my stuff to be ruined. Homes and businesses suffered great ruin from this flood. A friend of mine had an elite boutique in that area and she lost almost all of her merchandise as a result. Had I been one day late I can't even imagine the amount of money I would have to spend to replace my lost, plus there are some things that are unreplaceable. And if I had been a victim and lost most or all of my stuff, I trust that God would have helped me get over it and would have replaced all that I lost. Because He is in the restoration, renewing and replacing business. And He has done so much for me in the past, until it is hard to doubt Him.

In writing this book I have tried to tell it all but He has done so many many things for me over all these years, my memory fails me. Then God will have me, read something, I've written in the past or have a conversation or He will just bring to my memory what He wants me to share.

Divine Protection

As I write these wonderful testimonies, composing this book, I am enjoying myself because my heart is filled with so much joy. Enabling me to remember all the experiences I've had with God blessing me. Some testimonies make me cry, all of them make me rejoice and some make me laugh. Because when God displays His sense of humor it is so special. Actually, this testimony contains all three emotions. In the past, the cars I owned got replaced when I started to have enough trouble that showed me it's time to replace it. I had this car that was a good make and model that lasted longer than my cars in the past. So, when it started to give me trouble, I started to get things fixed, plus at the time I wasn't ready to buy a new car yet. After getting a couple of major problems fixed, the small problems started to happen. One day I went through a drive through and after I got my food the electric window would not go up. I said to myself, "that's ok because I park in the garage anyway. That was soon abandoned because what about during the day when I'm at work? Back to the "oh no!" I began to hit the switch and the window went up about ¼ of an inch. I said, "thank You Jesus". I kept hitting the switch and the window went up another ¼ inch. It kept going up about ¼ of an inch each time I would press the switch, so each time I kept saying "thank You Jesus". This went on for about 15 "thank You Jesus", until the window went completely up to the top. I said, "Lord You could have let the window up in one flip of the switch but You wanted my praise".

Ok now Sylvia, remember to never let your window back down, remember it is broken. A month or so later I was out shopping, and when I got back in the car, I pulled the seatbelt over me, but it only came halfway. It would not come all the way across my body nor retract. "Now what?" So now I had enough room to pull it halfway across my body and put my right arm in the loop and cover my right arm with my jacket so it would appear like my seat belt was intact. ("Sylvia trust Me and buy yourself a new car." "But wait Lord not yet I'm not ready"). Who did I think I was? Anyway, this went on for a while. Ok problem number three. Rainy season came along, and I turned on my windshield wipers one day on my way home from work. The wiper on the passenger side worked but not the driver's side. Not "Oh no", but "Oh Brother". "Not yet Lord I'm getting ready but I'm not there yet."

I love listening to the radio or a CD while driving and one day I popped in a CD and it was muffled and didn't sound right until it stopped playing the CD altogether. So now I was forced to listen to the radio all the time and not my CD's. My antenna would retract when I turned the radio off, and I had to remember that when I went through the carwash. Yep, you guessed it I forget to do this, I went through the carwash, the water started pouring on my car and when the carwash brushes began to wash my car, I heard this metal sound clanging against my car. I had forgot to turn the radio off, the brushes began to sway back and forth, and they hit my antenna, bent it and left it flopped over on the car. Bye bye radio. No radio, no CD player. But the straw that broke the camel's back was the radiator started leaking. So, every day I had to put water in it to be able to get back and forth. My son said "Mom I know a mechanic who would be able to fix the radiator". I told him I was not going to put another dime in that car.

A few days later my son and I were visiting family and it came time to go home. It was at nighttime and when we got ready to go it was raining. I said we cannot go now, let's wait until the rain stops because of the wiper situation. When it stopped raining, we ran to the car and left. When we got to the bridge toll gate, my son said, "do you smell that?" I said "no". He then rolled down the window and said, "you just blew your engine." Oh boy, oh brother oh no! He said "get off the bridge." Well at the point of the bridge where I was, the next turn-off was about ¼ mile. So, I just prayed, kept my feet on the gas pedal and the car kept going until it reached the first area to pull over safely to the side of the road. It was about midnight and very dark where we were. I was so glad my son was with me at the time. I called the tow company and we waited a long time because they had trouble finding us, plus it was so dark where we were. But they finally found us and took us home along with my car, so now it is time to get rid of the car. The next day I went to the dealership and bought me a new car, one that I loved and of course could comfortably pay for.

Even out of all the signs God gave me telling me to buy a new car, He still was merciful and gracious enough to not let me get hurt in my falling apart car. I wasn't faithless nor rebellious, I just had a plan and God allowed me to carry out my plan.

Luke 12:42 says, "And the Lord said, who then is that faithful and wise steward whom the Lord shall make ruler over his household, to give them their portion of meat in due season?"

I have always appreciated everything that God has done for me. Even after a hard trial I can look back, if not then, but sometime later and thank God for being there with me. After my mother passed away, I was able, shortly afterwards, to thank Him for not letting her suffer in a long illness. After my first marriage ended, I was thankful that we could remain friends. After my second marriage to my abusive husband ended, I was able to forgive him and move on. Thank You Lord for keeping me from getting hurt in an accident in that falling apart car. Every time I pass that area of bridge and I look at that tiny island where I was able to pull over to safety, I get teary eyed thinking about how God protected me and allowed my car to run just long enough to reach that island. God is patient and will let you carry out your plan so you can get out of the way of His bigger plan for your life.

Abusive Marriage, But I Got A Plan

I have a lot of compassion for the men and women who find themselves in an abusive relationship and/or marriage. Especially those who feel trapped or scared to make a move for the better. And especially for those who feel that this is the lifestyle they have to live in for the rest of their lives. People who have never been abused or who are not abusive don't know what it is like to be in that situation. All they can offer is their advice which in a lot of cases are hard to take. The most effective thing they can do is pray for you. An abuser is a cruel, selfish person and do not see where they are wrong. Some abusers are closet abusers because they show no signs of being abusive but behind closed doors it is another story. Some are so mean and blatant they don't care who knows and may be aggressive with you in front of other people, except family members. As forestated, on-lookers or non-abusive people don't realize how traumatic it is to the victim. I have even had someone who should have known better to say that physical abuse is worse than mental abuse. So, you know they didn't know what they were talking about.

"Why don't you leave?" Answer "It's not that easy". "Go back home to mama". Answer "No because she is not that supportive because my father abuses her", or you do not want her to know. "Go to a shelter". Answer "I have no money, or he'll find me, or I don't want to leave my stuff". In a lot of cases, an abused person always has an "excuse" but I thank God my situation never got that far because I was/am a praying person and I wasn't going to let it get that far. Nevertheless, there was some abuse in the 17 months that I was married to him. During the time we were dating there were no signs of him being abusive. Had there been I would not have married him. But as soon as I said, "I do", I should have said "I don't, or I can't" because there was an immediate change in him. Not towards him being abusive but a change in him, which I picked up right away. It was as if the words "I do", was etched in stone, like some seal of no getting out.

The first time, and only time, he slapped me was after we had been married about five months and it was because I didn't want to get up at 8:00 o'clock to cook breakfast on a Saturday, I wanted to get up an hour later. At that time, I was 52 years old and had never been hit that hard in my face ever. In fact, I don't ever remember being hit in my face at all. Listen being slapped that hard, you do see stars and hear bells. I could not believe what had just happened to me. I was driving at the time, when he slapped me, later that day and he was still talking about the breakfast incident. While he was ranting and raving, I said not one word. We were on our way to dump some boxes and the dumpsters were located in a large open field where there were no people present. I was wearing glasses at the time and after seeing where we were, I thought there are no witness so he may hit me again, so I took off my glasses, so if he did, hit me nothing would happen to my eyes. I thought "no one is around, he may hit me again, so take off your glasses Sylvia, get your butt whipped and when we get home bash him in the head with your cast iron skillet, and rolling pin." God was on his side because He knew my plans and God was more on my side because He knew I was capable of carrying out my plan and would possibly go to jail.

He did not hit me. Good for him.

I repented for marrying this man because somewhere I missed something. I saw subtle things but not enough. I was prayerful, at the time, but I still missed something, somewhere. One thing I can say is I knew I was way more advanced in the Lord and in the Word than he and we were unequal in our Christian walk and that is not really what I wanted in a new husband. But he pursued trying to get to know me. Every Sunday after church he would try to talk to me and I would rush him off. He was not what I was looking for and as a matter of fact I wasn't looking. He wasn't my "type" but eventually we exchanged phone numbers and it went from there.

Proverbs 18:22 – Says "Whoso findeth a wife findeth a good thing and obtain favor of the Lord".

This scripture is for a man not the woman. A woman does not look for or find a wife, but the man does. Like I said I wasn't looking in the first place. After church he would walk me to my car and ask me what I was going to do. I would always say I was going home to my son, and that was an excuse because my son was a grown man. I guess he never thought, "well if she is going home to her son, he must be a child, but she never brings him to church." I crack up every time I think about that. Single Godly women should stay very prayerful and wait on God if you want a husband. God knows if He has a husband for you. He knows who he is and where he is and when the time is right. Do not rush your life and don't rush God. And always stay open that God may not have a husband or another husband for you.

Do not be anxious, and do not be impatient and be content in whatever state that you're in. *Philippians 4:11 says, "Not that I speak in respect of want for I have learned in whatsoever state I am, therewith to be content"* Learn to be content with being single and learn to be content that you may be single for the rest of your life. It happens and it will continue to happen, that God just might desire for some of us to remain single. Let no one match make for you. Hear God and know His voice. I am saying this for a reason. The pastor, at that time, knew this man longer than I did and he also knew that I was "seasoned" in God and that I was not a babe in Christ and that I was gifted, have a calling on my life and more advanced even more than he, the pastor, that is. He also knew this man was a "babe" in the Lord. The man kept asking him about me and he finally told him to talk to me. He should have told him, man this lady is out of your league and have never gave an indication that she was looking for anyone.

OK. Stop right there! I am not saying the marriage was the pastor's fault, no it was my fault. I take full responsibility. What I am saying is the pastor should have been more of a pastor to us by telling him not to talk to me and why and he should have told me the man had an interest in me and not to give this man the time of day and why. Instead of trying to make himself look good in helping his friend. He was not a good pastor in protecting me and not a good pastor in growing up his sheep first before trying to get him a wife. I am not mentioning any names or real names in this book but if this former pastor ever read this book, he will know who he is and what I just wrote, I would say to his face. Plus, I am not mad at him either, we all make mistakes and I have forgiven him, whether he knows it or not. Because you learn from your mistakes and life experiences.

Romans 8:28 speaks of all things working together for our good is so true. Had I not married this joker; I would not know what I know now. I would not be able to help other women and men at the level I am at now, who are being abused. Oh yes, I could have learned this in another way, but this is the way God chose to teach me, and I am sure it was in a more effective way. As time went on things got worse, the physical abuse was grabbing and pushing but things escalated to verbal and mental abuse, which at times could be worse than physical. I thank God every day for making me strong because the mental abuse was not effective, and the verbal abuse got on my last nerve. He would rant and rave about anything and nothing. If I said two words, he had 99 words for each of my words. Just on and on and at this point all of what he was saying then is just a blur, I could not tell you what he was saying, if my life depended on it. One day I was praying, and God said, "Sylvia don't say a word." OK Lord I won't, and I didn't. I timed his ranting and raving one time and he went on one night for six hours. I just sat there with a shaking my head attitude. A lot of preachers can't go on for two hours. My Lord!

I was always prayerful, so I began to pray even longer. I know I got myself in this and after I repented, I said, "Lord you got to get me out". I knew prayer was my power tool in this dilemma. After dinner, a little TV and my bath, I would go to bed. Let me let you know this right now, not once was I afraid to get in the bed with him and sleep. I just knew that God would protect me and not let him hurt me, and God did just that. Sometimes, while in a deep sleep he would say really loud, "what do you want from me?" (in my mind I would think not a damn thing!). I would wake up with "what?" "What are you talking about?". In my head my answer was "I want absolutely nothing from you but for you to disappear and just go away and be part of my history, of a bad nightmare.

So, I just spent a lot of time in prayer. The weapons of our warfare are not carnal. 2 Corinthians 10:4 says, so that is why I did not tell my family members what I was going through. They would have dealt with him in a carnal way, which would have been justified by then. And this man would have come up dead, missing or a vegetable. And for the record, no one in my family is a murderer or a vicious person but he would have been dealt with in an ungodly way. No one in anyone's family will tolerate a family member being abused, I don't care who it is. I knew this was my battle and I had to let God fight for me. Plus, when you know scripture, you are held accountable for what you know and of course God knows what you know. It is not easy to step out of scripture. That's like getting to the toll gate and keep driving through and not paying the toll, you will get a letter sooner or later with a picture of you zooming through showing your license plate with a larger fine than what the toll would have cost you. Let's say you took a cooking class and are taught how to make nice fluffy biscuits and your teacher knows you know how to because she taught you well. When it comes time for the test and you make rock hard, burnt biscuits, the teacher has a right to give you a failing grade because she knows what you know. So, I knew how this battle was to be fought.

So, after being asleep for about two hours, maybe around 11:30 to midnight, God would wake me up to go pray. He would gently wake me up, and I would get up out of the bed as soon as I opened my eyes and go in the living room and pray. Sometimes I would pray from three to six hours. Yes, that's right and I would not fall asleep and had to go to work an hour away from where I lived. And I would stay awake the whole time praying in my heavenly language. The Spirit knows what to say to the Father in prayer and The Holy Spirit knows what you want to say. We are limited when praying in English because there is so much, we have to remember, so many scriptures we want to quote that doesn't come to mind, but The Holy Spirit knows your heart and your thoughts. That is why you should embrace the leading of The Holy Spirit. I thank God for that experience of praying that long, because that kind of trial takes that kind of prayer life.

I would fall on my knees at night with a small blanket over my head and when I would finish it would be daylight and I never knew that the daylight had come in. You would think if a person is cutting up, abusing a person or being mean to a person that is praying that much that they would straighten up. No not that Joe Booger, he got worse, so you see what kind of demon I was dealing with. There is a whole lot more to this story but, at this point, I am going to save that for another book. Yeah yeah, I know, you want some more juice but that will come later. My prayer life increased and although I was in this horrible situation, I was loving my time with God. One Friday night he did not come home, and he calls me and said he was coming home but I did not care if he did or not. On Saturday I had an all-day class and when I got home, he wasn't there yet. I would do anything to not be around him. At that time, I was willing to take a how to wash dishes or how to brush your teeth class just to be away. He called again that night saying he was coming home. At this time, and I hate to say this, but this is what I was hoping. I was hoping the police would knock on my door and tell me he was dead. I was hoping the hospital would call me and tell me he was hurt and dying. I was hoping the coroner would call and say come identify his body. That's how bad it was and it is so sad when a person can treat you so bad, and never let up, for no reason until you stop liking that person and don't care what happens to them. You can love a person but dislike some of the things they say and do. You can be in love with a person and dislike their habits. You can even be in love with a person but dislike them. But when you cause a person to stop liking and loving you, well that's pretty bad. Now when I prayed, I did pray for his soul, but I did not pray for him to change towards me. I did not want him to change for me or put up a front that he has changed. I wanted him out of my life forever. Please go your way sir and I will go mine.

During that Saturday, night I called my bank and found out that $400.00 had been withdrawn in $100.00 increments and this was crucial, so I knew then some major changes had to be made. He finally came home Sunday morning. And he asked me to do him a favor and not go to church, whatever that was about, I don't know. I had already made up my mind that I was not going to go to church because I was too tired from a lack of sleep. Not because of him, but because of it being hard to sleep soundly in that large house alone. He came in the room and said, "I'm going to call my father and talk to him about what I have done." And I am thinking "man we are two overgrown people, not teenagers and what can talking to your father do?" I have been talking to my Father and brother it's about to be over very soon". He could have called the Pope. He could have called the President of the United States. He could have called T. D. Jakes, that I love and respect so dearly or even called on God, it is too late, it was over. In my Sophia from The Color Purple voice, "fine with me", call whomever you wish. Stick a fork in my brother, I am done.

He didn't go to work Monday or Tuesday so that meant we were losing money because he didn't get paid for days off. We probably said two words to each other. I was numb, tired and so over this marriage. There was no way I was going to allow him to bring me down or rob me of what, I had worked so hard for. When my first marriage ended, I promised God and some more responsible people that I would never let another man bring me down, mentally, spiritually or financially. When I came home from work on Wednesday before I could put the key in the door, he flung the door open with a big grin, in a playful way. I guess that was supposed to change things. I just looked at him thinking "partner it's over". It was over, it was done, and I didn't care. I said nothing when I changed my clothes. I cooked dinner and we sat there at the table in silence. Then he said, "I'm going to Bible study with you tonight". "Aw man I did not want that to happen, you haven't been going". I thought. These are my friends, my sisters and my Bible study, my safe haven and my city of refuge. And I did not want him around my friends I knew before I met him. Don't give me that false fake attitude of now you are going to change, it's over buddy. Remember I don't like you or us anymore. I have had enough, and I am not one of those weak, desperate, scared, insecure women you know about, I am Sylvia, a child of God, were my thoughts.

Now about three weeks before all of this took place, I had shared with my first husband, who was one of my mentors, what I was going through and he was one who was praying for me and he hated that I was going through this. I told him that I had been obedient to God's will and instructions. I prayed, I kept my mouth shut when I was being badgered and I did not tell my family members, and nothing was happening. He said, "have you told God how you feel" I said "no". He said, "then you have a secret from God". Now we know God knows all but we also know or should know that God wants us to talk to Him, just like we would with our parents. And even though we may be afraid to tell our parents what's on our minds we should not be afraid to tell God what's on our mind. I was happy for that information and I had the perfect place and time. Where I worked and lived, I had two highways I could take to get to work and back. I usually took the same road going to work but sometimes I would take San Pablo Dam Road going home because it was up high in the hills and you could see the beautiful Dam and you may almost every day, see one of the beautiful deer, the possums and the racoon even an undesirable skunk. I did care about running into the animals and for the record I never hit one critter, almost, but never. I just loved driving on that road. So soon as I got to the top, I started yelling and said "God I have been going through this trial a long time. I have repented. I have kept my mouth shut like You told me. I have told no one in my family who would deal with him in a carnal way. I have even increased my prayer time with You up to and possibly over six hours, which I thoroughly enjoy. And You have done nothing". The Lord said, "Yes you are right, you Sylvia have to take that step of faith. You got to trust me and leave, leave everything. He is not going to leave. You got to make the first move". I heard Him very plain. I didn't say "Wait Lord leave my stuff. Take a step of faith. Trust You?" I said "OK" I was very happy with my instructions. I didn't know when, but I was glad I knew what to do.

All I secured was my book of poems, I had written over the years. It is hard to replace creativity and had I lost those poems it would be very difficult for me to replace them. I put my book of poems in the trunk of my car. Now back to the Bible study night. After we finished eating in silence, he got up from the table. I cleaned up the kitchen and began to redress for Bible study. He was watching TV. When I was in the bathroom combing my hair he came in there, stood at the door and said, "I don't know what's wrong with you, but you are walking around here, saying nothing". I thought, "you don't know what's wrong with me, man get real. Look in the mirror. The person you will see is what's wrong with me. The 17 months I have lived with you is what's wrong with me.

The pushing, the shoving, the badgering, the grabbing, the jealousy of my sons, the fakeness when you are around others. The wasting of money, among other things, not to mention the slap. Or did you forget the slap, I did not? That's what's wrong with me. Now all of that is a bit much on a 17-month marriage resume. I looked at him and I said, "I don't know what to say and I don't have anything to say". When something is dead, it is dead. He went back in the room. After I finished getting ready, I went in the room where he was and asked if he was going to Bible study. He looked at me with so much hatred and he caught himself, because he gave a quick gesture like he was going to throw the remote control at me. He didn't and he didn't have to answer, I knew the answer and I thought there you go with that fakery again.

I left, got into my car and as I was driving I began to say to God, "I have had to deal with a drunk Bobby (not his real name), and I have had to deal with an angry Bobby and when I get home I am going to have to deal with a drunk, angry Bobby, because I know he is going to go get something to drink, while I am gone and I will have to face him, but oh not tonight, not ever again, this is it. Little did he know that was my last night in that house and it would soon be his last few days in that house. At this point in this book this is told in detail because I want the readers, you, to see what God can and will do to get you out of a bad living situation. Abuse is not ordained by God and not to be tolerated or lived with. God will make you strong. God will bail you out. God will protect you while He is making you strong enough to get out of that bad situation and He will show you that it takes long hours of prayer and faith to do so. He will make the weak strong. He will make the doubter become full of faith and He will help you become more trusting in Him.

When I got to Bible study, which was, at my friend's house, I walked in, we all spoke, hugged and do all of the things you do when greeting each other. The hostess, who was not a pastor at the time, but is now, said, "OK let's get started and I will start with Sister Sylvia, I know she has something to say". Oh yes, I do! As I began to speak, the door opened, and more people began to come in and we went through the greeting thing again. Ok as I began to speak, more people came in, hugs, greets, again. I guess God wanted everybody to hear what I had to say. My friend laughs and said, "OK Sylvia let's start again because you must really have something to say". I was thinking, "you don't know the half of it". I began to speak and I said "I have been living in hell for 17 months and I have left my house, and I don't know where I am going to go because I am not going to go back". I was hit with from my left, "oh you're going home with me", then hit from my right, "sister you can stay with me, or me or me". Man can you feel the love tonight? I was totally embraced by some strong loving Sisters which is now a rare breed, but they do still exist. I felt so loved and cared for and protected. They stopped right then and there and said, "put Sylvia in the middle and let's form a circle around her". Then they put one sister in front of me and one behind me and began to pray. I will say it was at least twenty-five people there. I felt such joy that even right now I cannot explain. I felt supported and I felt protected because I had a place to escape. I had left all my "stuff". I loved that big beautiful house, the furniture and the neighborhood but it was just "stuff" and I didn't care. This was stuff God gave me and stuff that God could easily replace. Stuff.

I ended up staying at the hostess' house. I slept on her couch and she even slept on the couch close to me, instead of her bed just to give me that assurance that I was protected. As I slept, I got the best sleep I had ever had in months. Free at last. Around 4 AM my pager started "blowing up". It was him and I ignored every one of his pages, I was like "buddy you have no clue". I am not weak I am strong; I am not needy; I am fulfilled and I am God's precious daughter who is not to be abused by any man. God told me not to answer any of his pages, let him wonder. God told me there is no conversation and there is absolutely nothing to talk about. I often wonder what he would have said, had I answer. He probably would have said he was sorry and start crying. But I have heard that before and I have seen your fake tears before. He might even have said that he was not going to do what he has done ever again. And he would have said that I was his wife and what I was doing was not Biblical. Because he has said that before and lastly, he may have said some threatening words. But I have been there done that. I was so free. Free as a bird out of its cage.

What I am saying in this testimony is to help those who feel trapped or stuck. It only took me 17 months because I needed to experience what I did so I can help others. God knew He was going to equip me for the task. He knew it wasn't going to kill me and He knew in the midst of it all I would pray for Bobby, forgive him and move on. The next day I called my girlfriend who knew about what I was going through, and she had already opened her doors for me. I called my job and my supervisor was ever so understanding. He said, "take the time you need, and do what you have to do". I stayed at my friend's for about a week and her family treated me royally and her husband was incredibly supportive. Now let's get to the stuff. A few months before I left, his sister and brother-in-law paid us a visit and stayed with us for about a week. They were on their way to Hawaii to be stationed there and had to stop and see this woman (me) who had changed her brother. They told me in so many words that in the past he was a bad difficult person and thought I had changed him. I did not know this about him when I married him. Even his sister's husband said to me, "Sylvia you have no idea how he was", and I am thinking, "he hasn't changed either". Remember I told you he was a fake. He faked it all the while they were there. She had not been in communication with him because of how he was. In fact, his four other sisters and brother did not like him. Well she befriended me, and we would talk after I left. So, after they were settled in Hawaii, she would call me behind his back and also talk to Bobby. And it was revealed to her that he had not changed. So, she cared for my safety and wellbeing. She asked me one day, how we were doing, and I told her how miserable I was living with him.

She said she thought so and began to tell me she had started to see the signs of the "old" Bobby. She said, "if she had known me before I married him, she would have told me not to marry him". She was afraid for me, but I told her I know how to get out of the house without him knowing. I would be gone forever and I truly believe God was not going to allow him to hurt me because if he had hurt me badly when I got the strength, I had plans to off him myself. Even though as a Christian you hate to have to say these things, but a person can take so much. Plus, I knew God did not want me to fight this battle. That battle belonged to God. So, while I was gone. I did not answer his pages. His sister talked to both him and I and he did not know that she first told me he was angry. Then he got scared being in that big house alone. Then he left the house out of fear. When he was gone, she told me, plus by that time I had told my family everything. There's more to this part but I will fast forward to when I found out that he was gone out of the house, I got my family and friends together to help me put my stuff in the storages mentioned earlier.

When I had first entered the house, I saw where he had taken all of my clothes out the closet and piled them up in the floor like he was going to set them on fire, but somehow had second thoughts. Plus, the house was equipped with a sprinkler system. When I moved, I left all of his clothes, undamaged, which I could have destroyed but what was the point? Now I could have damaged his stuff and repent later. In court I got everything I mean everything. I got everything I came into the marriage with and everything I bought with money I made before I married him, thank God for that California law. After about 13 years later, one of my job functions was to look for "lost" people to try to reunite them with their minor children. So, I was equipped with systems and programs to search for people either by, name, date of birth or addresses. So, I decided to search for him and I found his phone number and I called him. He answered the phone not knowing at first it was me and when I told him who it was, he began praising God and thanking God that I had called. He wanted to tell me he was sorry and that there was nothing I had done to make him be like he was and he often think about where he would be in life had he not been such a terrible person. That phone call was for him not me because I had forgiven him a long time and had moved on. He needed to repent to me and say what he said. The phone number I called him from was a protected phone number that when you called it you would get a recording telling you that you are not able to reach anyone or even trace the number. And funny thing he had the nerve to asked could he call me at that number, while I am thinking "go ahead buddy knock yourself out"! Through it all I appreciate the fact that God kept His word, by protecting me and my belongings.

Failed Brakes At The Right Time

Some things in life we have to deal with more than once, like car problems or issues on our jobs, lack of finances, house problems, people problems and sickness just to name a few. We get over a cold then we battle the flu, we break a bone, have a toothache or back problems. It's always something but let's talk about the car. Somewhere along the line of owning a car you are going to run into some kind of car problem. Thank God they are making cars better and better but even the best running car can run out of gas, but what about brakes, you ask. This brings me to my next testimony of how God blessed me in another car situation. Coming home from work one day, as soon as I pulled in front of my house I heard a squeaky sound when I pressed my foot on the brake and the car almost did not stop, but it did right in front of my house and I had just traveled well over 15 miles from work on these, about to go out brakes. And the beauty of this testimony is I had a mechanic who was a close friend, that was able to come to my house, install new brakes and I did not miss a day of work. Won't He do it?!

Letting Your Supervisors Have It

We who are children of God always want to do better and be better people. That is one of our main prayers, plus we pray that family and friends do/be better. There was a time I was praying that God change a person, but as I continued to pray this prayer, I felt guilty and judgmental. So, I asked God can I pray this prayer and He said we can pray for others to change for the better and I felt better about praying this way. He said everyone want to do better and that keeps my prayer from being judgmental. I was being assigned a different supervisor from what I had because our office was making changes. They switched me over to a supervisor that was not liked and had a bad reputation.

Different co-workers would come over to me and say that they had heard I was going to report to Tommy (not his real name) and they felt bad for me. They said he was selfish, only cared about himself and hard to work for. They wanted to know how I felt about working for him. I said that I have always gotten along with my supervisors over the past 25 years and I had no problem so as far as I know things will be alright.

My function was to pull my reports for him first thing, in the morning, answer the phone and assign work to the technicians. Answering the phones was shared with the other clerks, but not my other duties. So, everything was running smooth and I did my job promptly and correctly. Only one time all of the information was captured in the morning report and it was the end of the day and I was about to leave for the day. I had on my coat and my purse was on my shoulder and he stopped me at the door. He told me there was information that was missing, and he needed a new report. So, I came back into the office, took off my coat, logged back on, pulled the report, gave it to him and left for the day. Sometimes I would be on the phone and he would stop at my desk, interrupt me and ask me if I was on a personal call. If it were a personal call I would say "yes is there something you need me to do?" And he always said "no". That in itself was annoying, but I would just let it go. A few months went by and then the wrong thing happened on the wrong day. It was that time of the month all women go through and I had spent a lot of time in the lady's room. After about my third trip to the lady's room, when I returned to my desk, there was a post-it-note on my phone from him saying "see me".

When I went to his office, he said "I have been to your desk three time and each time you were not there". I said, "it's that time of the month, do you want me to let you know every time I need to change"? Oh, he threw his hands up as if he wanted to cover his ears, (Lol) and said "I don't need to hear this". I said, "well you asked". He got quiet and I went to my desk. By this time, I was upset terribly upset until I was also angry and crying and probably angry because he made me mad enough cry. I called another co-worker across the way (same room) and he could tell that I was upset. He was upset because I was upset. He said, "Sly what's wrong?" and I told him what happened. He said that is straight up harassment, and that I need to file a grievance. I said I will and I looked for the union steward. I found him outside and after telling him the story he said, "yes let's file a grievance".

I was upset because I knew I did my job well, with no mistakes and promptly and I was honest with him if I was on a personal call. Hey, I knew and know Christ and I tried to do those things that is pleasing in His sight and reflect Jesus Christ, as the scripture says. After I filled out my gradience forms I was still upset. When I am upset and or angry, which is rare, I pace because I cannot keep still, or think or relax. Well he saw me pacing, probably like a caged lion (Lol) and he said, "Hey Sly can we talk?" and I said "yes". And we went into the conference room and he closed the door. I said, "do I need to get a union representative?' He said, "no I thought we could settle this ourselves". Now see what kind of person he was, did not want anyone else in on this to show what kind of person he really is. I could not stop crying and he said, "maybe I should leave you and let you get yourself together". I said, "no sit here and watch me cry" (so dramatic). So, he waited. I began to tell him what everyone was saying to me when they found out I was going to be reporting to him. How terrible, he is and how selfish he is and so hard to work for. I told him I had no problem, having to work for him and how I have done my job on time, correctly and was honest with him. How he had stopped me while going home to pull some last-minute report for him without a complaint. And he never said one word to me about my work, nor ever had any complaints. He apologized profusely and said he should have never said anything about me being away from my desk, knowing it must be for a good reason and that I can always be found at my desk unless I am on a break, at lunch or in the ladies room. And even then, he needed nothing from me at the time.

This man was visibly shaken and nervous and kept expressing how sorry and wrong he was. Everything calmed down and the meeting was over. Soon after that he went on vacation. Now that was timely. Apparently, word got around the office (small office about 65 people), what had happened. After his vacation he was temporarily assigned to another office, another timely move. And while he was gone one of his peers came to me and said, "I don't know what you said and what went on in that room, but Tommy is a changed man. They had been working with him for years and never seen him so humble'. They said, "Sly you have changed him". I told them that he pushed me to tell him about himself and when he returned you could tell he was a changed person and he treated me better and with respect.

A few months later in that same office, I had a similar encounter with yet another supervisor. This supervisor had that same hard to get along with, bossy personality, that most subordinates didn't care for. This one was a few years younger and also had to go on military duty from time to time, so he had that attitude of bossing everyone around in an unfavorable way. That attitude of "get yourself together because if you don't, I will see to it that you do because I am in charge". Somedays you didn't know if you should shake his hand or salute him. He was not my immediate supervisor, but he was the only supervisor that came in at 5:00 AM and I was the only clerk that came in at 6:00 AM, so he was my manager for an hour until my own supervisor came in at 7:00 AM.

I would get to work around 6:00 am, log in, leave my desk for coffee and water then return to my desk to start my day. After doing this for a few weeks or so, he came and got me and told me we needed to talk. I asked him if I needed a union rep and he said no. He then began asking me, in a semi-yelling manner "what is this ritual you have every morning that you can't be at your desk at 6:00?" I told him what I would do and he said, "you are supposed to be at your desk at 6:00 not 6:05", that he needed me at my desk on time. I apologized and said I would come in early enough to be on time to work and let him know he was right. He kept going on after he had made himself clear and would not leave it alone. See what he did not know, was what I knew.

"You are supposed to be on time if you are not ready to work at 6:00 you are considered late", he kept yelling. OK already I got it. Finally, I said, "well I heard that you are always late every morning and you are never here, on time at 5:00 am". Then he got quiet and started explaining. "Well you see I live in Antioch and I have to travel Highway 4 and its rough". I said "I travel Highway 4 also, from the other direction as well. I know all about Highway 4 both ways. I used to live in Pittsburg, the city just before Antioch, so don't tell me nothing about Highway 4.

Then he said, "well Sly I am stressed from thinking I might get laid off when they make this next cut".

I told him that he made the decision to accept the position and he must deal with what may happen. He then apologized and I apologized again, and we shook hands and went back to our desks in peace. About two weeks later he came to my desk and said he was out and about and saw something he thought I would like. It was the cutest ceramic mask to add to my collection I had on my wall. I was delighted and thanked him and immediately hung it up. Every now and then one of my co-workers would come by my desk and notice my new mask and they would say, "oh I see you got a new mask". And I would tell them who gave it to me, and they would be in shock and say "what"? not him he never does anything nice for anyone. "Sly what did you do"? I didn't reveal what happened I just told them that we had a talk. From that day on he and I had a good relationship and he treated me with respect.

Let me get something straight, concerning these last two stories about these supervisors. I am not out to "straighten" out no one. And if something I say or have said will help someone to do better, I praise God for that and all the glory belongs to God. But when you live for Christ and you seek to please God in all you do, when the time comes God will come to your defense especially when you are under an attack. And God will give you that Holy boldness to speak up. Over the years God does bless us with wisdom and that wisdom is to be used by yourself and shared with others. That office was a mess before I came and a lot of the subordinates had to tolerate the bossing around and disrespect from their leaders, especially these two, but God stepped in and made some changes and I am glad He chose me to do some of His work.

Quick Healing Of My Grandson

My grandson is an adult now but from the time he was born and for many years after that he spent a lot of time with me. We are very close to this day and always will be. When he was a toddler somewhere around 1½ years old, he, his mom and I went to my storage to pick out some things. While his mother was going through some boxes, I was watching him. Well you know how toddlers love to run and he was no exception. While running he fell on the grated metal floor and cut his lip rather deeply. At the time, his mother did not know what had just happened. I picked him up because he was crying so I could take him to his mother and I already knew she was going to freak out. When she saw him, she screamed, and I was upset that he was hurt, too but I was calm. She was so out of it that I told her I

would take him to Children's Hospital which was a couple of miles away. I strapped him in and started talking to him like he was 12 years old. I began to tell him what had happened to him and letting him know that we were going to the hospital to see the doctor to fix his cut on his lip. He was so interested in what I was saying he stopped crying. I told him he had an accident and hurt himself and we needed to go to the doctor. I told him as we would approach the corner that I was going to make a turn and go a few blocks to the emergency room, and he listened as if he understood. Never underestimate a child.

When I took him to the window to register, the receptionist asked me if I was his mother, maybe because we have the same last name. I told her that I was the grandmother. Then she asked where the mother was, I said somewhere freaking out. She laughed and said it was ok that I brought him in place of the mother. She put us in a room and put the cutest little open back gown on him and said the doctor would be right in. I held him my arms to keep him calm and secure and he fell asleep, then I fell asleep. I know we were asleep for a good while and still no doctor. I carried my grandson to the front and told the receptionist that I had been waiting for a long time and no one has seen my grandson. She was shocked and apologized and said she thought we had been seen by a doctor and released a long time ago. Plus, it was an unusual slow night and the doctors didn't have much to do so she thought we were gone by then.

As soon as I got back to our room, in comes the doctor. Now the cut on his lip was from his nose down to his upper lip and ¾ of an inch long and was deep. The doctor looked at his lip and it had closed.

He kept turning my grandson head looking in all angles. He said, "let me go get another doctor". The two of them returned and after the second doctor examined him, they agreed that he needed no stitches. The hour we waited gave time for the cut to close and began to heal. Healed to the point that all he needed was some Neosporin. Had the doctor seen us as soon as we arrived the cut would have been fresh and would have caused them to put about five stitches in but the waiting cause the cut to close up and began to heal itself. We know Who did the healing. God of course. He set up everything to happened the way it did so my grandson would not have to go through the painful procedure of getting stitches which would later have to be removed and leave a lifelong scar which he does not have. What a mighty God we serve.

Social Security Blessing

Often times we will get in the mail information that we should read thoroughly but we will take a look at the document, knowing that it is of some importance and put it in a safe place. Then later in life we may be faced with a situation that was covered in that document and we have to go back and take a look at it to get a better understanding or call someone that you know who got the same document but read it thoroughly. Sometimes you wished you had read the document as soon as you got it because now you have a penalty or you may have short changed yourself by not reading it or sometimes you find out in the nick of time before something expired. This brings me to my next testimony, one with a beautiful twist.

We have heard over the years the phrase "He may not come when you want Him but He's always on time". Even though this isn't a scripture it is certainly true to a degree because even though they say He may not come when you want Him, there are times He does come when you want Him, because He is always here with us. This leads me to my next testimony of how my social security came when I wanted and needed it to. After a few years in my second major job we had problems with our computer, so they sent for a technician. He was extremely popular, and everyone was glad to see him. I did not know him, so this was my first time meeting him. People were calling him "short timer" because he was soon to retire. I asked him how long he had been with social services and he said about ten years, but he had already retired from the same large communication company I had retired from. I found out in our conversation that he and I had worked at the same location at the same time. He began to name people he had worked with, naming some people I knew. So, this was the beginning of our short-term friendship. So, every time he came in the building he would come over to my desk and we would have short conversations. One day I saw him in the hallway and he stopped me and said "Hey I found out that after I reach my full retirement age, I can draw my social security, still work and make as much money as I want". I was glad to hear this because I was approaching my full retirement age but I really wasn't aware of this information he just shared. I was thinking that I would start drawing my social security after I retired.

This is that information that was provided for me that I paid no attention to, but God saw to it that I was made aware of this, from almost a total stranger. See how God will put people in your life, for a season, to be a blessing to you? So, I called social security to see what I needed to do. I had just bought my first house a few years prior and was in desperate need of more income. When I called them, they said I had to call the year I was turning 65 to set things up so everything will be in place. I was turning 65 the next year in about eight more months. As soon as the next year came, I went into the SS office to set things in motion. The clerk told me I was too early since it was January and my birthday were coming in May. She told me I should do this in March. OK I had to wait. When March came, I called again, and I got a real nice lady who was willing to help me sign up. She asked me if I had 45 minutes and I said "yes". She began to process my claim and after all the questions she said when May came, I would be set and expect to see the money in my checking account. Then she said I could start now but I would lose some money if I did and she offered to see how much money I would lose. First of all, I was glad to even know I could start in a couple of months. After checking she said I would lose about $20.00 a month.

I was fine with that amount and told her. Then she said "oh I see that you came in the office in January and I could start from that time, but you will lose a total of $40.00 a month if I go back to January". I was fine with that because I needed for my social security to start right away, since it can. She told me that everything was in place and I would start receiving my deposits in my bank. This was on a Thursday. On Saturday I was dressing to get ready to run my errands. I heard the Lord say, "call your bank". What? I thought and I said, "why should I call my bank, I know what is in my bank, why should I call". After about five minutes the Lord said it again and I just said "OK, I will". Reluctantly, I picked up my cell phone and called my bank and the recording said I had over $3,000.00 in the bank. I immediately closed my flip phone in confusion and disbelief. I said to myself "something is wrong with my cell phone, let me use my land line. And yes, I called my bank on my land line and I had the amount the first phone call revealed. All I know is I had about $250.00 in the bank and now I was richer. It took just two days for the money to transfer to my bank. What I thought was going to happen in two months happened in two days. This change in income was a tremendous help and blessing so yes God blessed when I needed Him, and He blessed me on time. I also shared this information with you concerning Social Security so you will know some of how the process works if you are not receiving yours yet.

We Shall Be Witnesses For Jesus Christ

The moment you say yes to the Lord in acceptance to salvation He offers, is the same moment you are qualified as a witness. You can witness that a change has taken place in your life, and you have gone from lost to being found. You have this strong desire to tell others what took place. the transition, the freedom you experience and the gladness in your heart that takes place. You are already capable of being a witness, even with the minimum scripture knowledge, you may have, at that time. And as you start to remember and study scripture, you become a better witness. But sharing what knowledge and experience you have makes you able to witness.

I say all of this because over the years I have heard people say things like, "you got to really know scripture before you go out there and witness". Which is not true. That is one of the oldest tricks of the enemy. It is true that the more you witness the better you become. But is not that just about true about everything? Don't let the enemy stop you from being a witness for Jesus Christ because of fear. You are capable at any time in your life to be a successful witness. Telling and sharing with others what God has done for you, is a witness. Talking about those open doors, is a witness or that healing that took place, is a witness.

The following are just two of my awesome experiences in witnessing. Since I had, had experience in witnessing, the pastor asked me to teach a class on the subject. After weeks of teaching in demonstration and roll playing, I felt they were ready to start going out in the world and witness. Shortly after teaching the class, we had an outing at a local park, and we were supposed to passed out tracts and flyers and feed our congregation and anyone who cared to join us. This was just one of our community services. After getting settled, I said to two of the sisters, "let's go witness, and I'll show you how it's done".

The park was beautiful and about the size of two blocks square. As we approached different ones, I would offer to hand them a tract, telling them who we were and inviting them to our church and inviting them to eat if they wanted to. Letting them know that they were more than welcomed to join us. I then told them we were willing to pray for them, right then and there, if they like. Mostly all of them we approached were very kind and accepted our tracts and said they wanted us to pray for them in our prayer time. I remember out of all the people we approached, not person said, no. Most people said yes, they want us to pray and most people are kind and respectful. Sure, there are mean and hateful people out there, who want you out of their faces but the majority respects what we stand for.

As we were walking through the park, we spotted six young men standing on the corner. As we began to approach them, they saw us coming. Two of them broke away from the others and went across the street to the other corner. You could tell that they did not want to be bothered by us. These boys looked to be about 15 to 18, somewhere in that age group. I told them who we were and asked them if they wanted us to pray for them. One of the young men said, "yes you need to pray for him", as he pointed to one of his friends. I said, "why should we pray for him?" and the kid said, "because he keeps doing dumb things". So, I asked the kid who was being pointed to, "what are the dumb things you keep doing?" He shrugged his shoulders and said he didn't know. So, I said "ok we are going to pray for you right now, for you to stop doing dumb things. My two companions grabbed my hand as we grabbed the boy's hands to form a circle, right there on the corner, on the street. By that time, my eyes were closed, and my head was bowed. One of my friends began to nudge me on my arm and as I looked up, the two boys who had walked across the street had joined us in the circle and had bowed their heads. Oh Lord, did that bless my soul. I prayed and after praying three of them joined us for lunch.

At that moment, I realized that I don't care how young people may be tough, or tough acting, they all want protection. They may act like they do not want any part of prayer, or salvation, but deep within they don't want to die young and they do want someone praying for them.

Who those young men are, to this day, I don't know? Where they are, I don't know, but I do know that through that witnessing experience, a seed was planted, or a seed was watered and as the scripture says God gives the increase. I also thank God that the two sisters who were with me got a chance to see and experience part of what witnessing is all about. And see that it is not that hard and see how witnessing is so rewarding in many ways. I thank God for that experience.

Being attached to a ministry that make witnessing a part of their ministry is, utmost, it is epic. Once you get in the habit of witnessing with your fellow worshippers, you constantly have that feeling that you are doing your part in reaching the world, and the sense of doing your duty. Another ministry, I was involved in made witnessing one of their priorities. We would go every Saturday, in the neighborhood where our church was located, which was North Richmond. And if you know anything about North Richmond, you know that, that was known as one of the rough areas in the San Francisco Bay Area. At first, I wasn't too fond of that area, but after a few weeks, I was ok.

We should go and knock on the doors and pass out flyers and invite them to our church. We would also ask them if they want us to pray, they always would say yes, come on in. Some of them would call other family members who were in the back to come to the front and join us in prayer. I cannot say that a lot of them began to attend our church, that was not our mission. Our mission was to get the Word of God out about Jesus Christ and His shed blood for our salvation and deliverance. Some Saturdays we would stand on the corner, kitty cornered to an active crack house. Yes, you read right, and active crack house. At first, those who ran that house, looked at us, like they wanted us to leave, but after a few weeks, they saw that we were just going to sing and pass out flyers. And that is all we did, because our mission was to plant a seed or water a seed and let God give the increase. So never let anyone make you afraid to witness or share a word from the Lord, because that is our duty and our utmost mission, is to help save the lost and get the message out that Jesus loves them and want them to be with Him in eternal life.

Believe I Testify While I Have A Chance... My Three Lifetime Companions

Living for God is the most wonderful experience anyone can have. There is no comparison. You are serving the most powerful, loving, caring Being there is. God makes sure it will be a fantastic journey you will never regret and cannot forget. He gives you written promises you can hold Him to keep. He provides for you and gives you the resources you need to live for Him. I can go on and on about how great God is. I have shared in this book just a few of the wonderful things God has done. While living for Christ you will began to experience His blessings in many forms. That is how God is. Closed doors swing wide open. Closed doors open unexpectantly. Some no's become yes and some yeses against you become no's. Healing takes place. Ways start to be made. Those things that seems impossible became possible. Things just start to happen to let you know that God is all in it. God's blessings become so enjoyable till you cannot wait for the next one. When a situation comes up you wonder how God is going to handle it, especially after you have given it to God.

In 2003 I had the most wonderful, supernatural experience of my entire life and so far, nothing has topped it. It is when my Three Companions made me aware that they are with me. It was the night of January 3, 2003. I went to bed as usual; it was a Friday night. Sometime in the

104

middle of the night I was awaken because I felt the presence of someone in my room. I was in a vision. My grandson Jewel was in the bed with me. He physically was not there but he was present in the vision. I was a little startled from these three beings in my room and my grandson assured me that everything is alright and will be alright because he was there with me. He was about 16-17 at the time and it is his nature to be protective. We were laying in an angle across the bed on our backs. As I looked up to the ceiling there was this small angel hovering over my head. He (no gender) was about the size of a bed pillow. He had the most beautiful face I have ever seen. His complexion was like soft pink over white alabaster. He communicated to me that he was my guardian angel and the angel that communicates to me what God wants me to know and that he was the carrier of all the blessings God has for me. He was very pleasant and easy to look at. He never took his eyes off of me and always looked at me directly in my eyes. His face was incredibly beautiful and reminded me of a baby with chubby cheeks. It was hard for me to stop looking at him.

The second angel was standing by the middle of my bed and he was about 5'6", and I didn't know who he was and he didn't communicate anything to me, but I knew he was harmless and loving. The third angel was standing in my doorway and he was very tall, and his body filled entire doorway. He communicated to me that he was my angel of warfare and he would protect me from harm. They were in my room for a while then they ascended through the roof leaving three perfectly round holes in the ceiling and this soft flowing fabric hanging from each hole. That was the end of the vision. I slept until the morning and when I awoke, I had no memory of what happened in the middle of the night with these angels.

I went about my day with my Saturday ritual of cleaning and going to the store for groceries. At the time I lived downstairs in the back where you had to walk or drive down this sloped driveway which put me directly in front of my door. From time to time someone would be in the driveway and I would have to blow my horn so whoever it was would come and move their car which should not have been there in the first place. Well when I came home, you guessed it, someone was blocking me. This time it was the handyman who was working on the house next door and should have parked next door. My landlord owned both properties and he would park in the driveway sometimes. When I saw his car, I was livid because I could not see where he was to tell him to move and I had a lot of groceries. That meant I had to park on the streets and make several trips down this driveway to unload my groceries and my son was not home to help me. After my third trip and last time I was dead tired, angry and I really didn't want to say anything to the handyman at that time, if I found him, because he was a nice guy and I was too mad to deal with him. So, I just flopped on my bed and began to cry and say, "God he knows people live back here and park back here and the house he is working on next door has its own driveway, why did he park in my driveway. And who were those angels in my room"? That is when that vision hit me because I had totally forgotten about the vision. I have heard that people call that an "open vision". I don't know.

This hit me sometime in the middle of the day when everything dawned on me. Right away I began to relive the whole thing. Every detail came back to me. I went over each moment, step by step. I then told the Lord, that I know who the first and third angels were, but I needed to know who that middle angel was. It is my understanding that a dream may need an interpretation, but a vision does not.

Meaning, the meaning is clear as the vision happened, I just did not know who the middle angel was.

This started the pace of a fantastic journey.

I shared my experience with my ex-husband, first husband, father of my sons. Remember the "good ex", my very close friend in spite of and he said, "maybe he is a healing angel". Mmm sounds good to me. So, I began to check in one of my Angel books and came upon the healing angel Raphael. But I could not find enough information about him. I did all the researching I could but still was not satisfied. Now I am on a mission. Who is this angel Raphael? One night while in bed watching TV, this commercial came on and it said, "A little piece of Heaven, Pinole's Bible bookstore". I thought, "what is this Bible bookstore, that I don't know about that's about a mile from my house"? I thought I knew about all the local Bible bookstores. I got the address and hoped, when I went there, they would have something on Raphael. The next day or so when I went to that store, when I pulled up in front of the store, I said to myself, "oh I see why I don't know about this bookstore it's a Catholic bookstore." Now keep in mind I don't have a thing against Catholics, I love them like I love everybody else, and some of my closest friends are Catholic. Plus, I knew that God lead me to this store, and I am not going to let anything stop me, I am on a mission.

I went in and there was an older gentleman in the store, and he asked me could he help me. I began to tell him about my vision that I had, and I was looking for some information on angels. He said, "this is all I have", and it was a small book, a little larger than a deck of cards, about 35 pages, entitled "Raphael", and all he had was that one copy. And the book cost $2.95. I got really excited and let me add this, when I was telling him about the vision, he listened very attentively and did not act like I was crazy. A very nice man, that I appreciated for listening. I learned that not only is Raphael the healing angel, but he is the angel of good marriages and the traveling companion angel that protects you when you travel. I believed he has more duties, but this is what I learned from this book. As soon as I learned about Raphael things started to happen. OK readers it's time for you to put on your seatbelts.

At this point, I am not concerned if you disbelieve but I sure hope you do, because it will bless your soul. And do not think that I have gone off the deep end because I haven't. And if this vision and revelation of it had not happened to me, I probably would be a skeptic too. You believe according to where you are in God and what your personal experiences, with Him has been. So many wonderful things began to happen to me after finding who these angels are and why they were told by God to reveal themselves to me, but I love having this experience in my life. So many wonderful blessings have been in my life but next to salvation, this tops it all.

I have shared this with some people who have said they wished this had happened to them. Thank You God for blessing me this way. It gets hard sometimes to write or share this experience without stopping to cry and praise God. One day when I got off work and I was on my way home about 15 minutes away, I decided to go home through the city instead of hopping on the freeway and hopping right off. When I get about five minutes from my house my car went dead right at the red light. It was early evening, but it was dark outside already. Immediately this lady tapped on my passenger window and said, "don't worry I will stay with you until help arrives. Do you need me to do anything?" I rolled down the window and said, "yes help me find my tow service number in my phone, because I don't have my readers and I can't see the small print on my phone". She found the number and I called them. She said she would wave off cars, so I won't get hit. This was heavy commute time, and everybody is trying to get home or to their destination.

After a few minutes, the highway patrol drove up. He asked me had I called for help and I told him I had. He said, "well call them back". When I did, he took the phone and said, "this is officer so and so and your client Ms. Jackson is stuck in a dangerous area and if you don't send someone out right away, I will have tow her away and impound her car". He then hung up after saying goodbye and gave me my phone. Then he said, "I can't tow and impound your car because you have stopped, I just told them that to make them hurry up", with a chuckle.

Then he said, "you need to get out of your car before someone not paying attention could accidently run into you". So, I got out of my car. He then said, "no don't stand here on the street I don't want anyone to try to snatch your purse". I was in front of Denny's and there were two employees standing outside taking a smoke break. The officer said to them, "this is Ms. Jackson and I need you to let her wait inside until her tow truck arrives because I don't want her on the street, where she can possibly get hurt", and they said "OK". So, while I am sitting waiting for the tow truck to come, this huge tow truck pulls up, so I go outside. He says, "is this your car?" I said "yes". He said, "get in so I can push it up further to get it out of the way". I said, "no are you with Farmers?" He said "no", but I want to help you get out of the way". I told him no because if you do that then Farmer's won't see me here and they are looking for me to be in front of Denny's he said "oh". Now I thought he was going to drive off, but what he did was take his huge tow truck and backed it up so he could park behind my car to protect it and waited there. I thought he would get offended because I refused his help. But if I had let him push me up further a half a block to the side, not only would Farmer's not see me but it would put me back on the street, out in the open, taking me away from the safety of being inside Denny's, but he just sat in his big old tow truck.

Shortly after that Farmer's came. The big tow truck guy gave me a friendly wave and smile as he drove off. Farmer's towed me home and then the driver, after doing his paperwork, said, "wait I want to check something". He raised my hood up and said, "Ma'am, it's your battery, you just need a new battery that's all". The next morning before work I went and bought a new battery and my car started right up. I asked the Lord what was that all about and I never knew a battery could just quit while in motion. The Lord said, "I just wanted you to see what I could do". Wow all that protection and help from one incident. Raphael, the angel of travel.

The next thing that happened was really strange. One time in the middle of the night I woke up on my stomach with my head hanging off the bed and I wondered how I got in that position. Because I am a side sleeper, not one who sleeps on their stomach. Upon turning myself over I inhaled through my nose and I heard all this rattling in my nose. "What?" I blew my nose and it filled the tissue with blood, thick blood. So, I concluded that something happened in my head during the night and the angel turned me over so I would not choke on my blood. Thank You Father. And that never happened again. Raphael the healing angel.

Some testimonies are more powerful than others, larger than others, longer than others but all of them bring so much joy. As I write I have to stop and praise God for all He has done. I must stop, periodically and shed tears of joy. Tears of gratefulness of this wonderful journey, God has allowed me to be on. Am I perfect and is this the reason I have such experiences in God? No not by a long shot. God is just that good, gracious and merciful to us and He wants us to know about Him and see the wonderful things He has in store for us.

Peter is one of our prime examples of God using and blessing the "imperfect". Peter was someone to reckon with, he lied, denied and tried Jesus' patience, but he did walk on water and he was very instrumental in the beginning of the early church, being present in the dispensation of the Holy Ghost. One of the most powerful places to be. And in all of the negative things Peter did do, nevertheless he was used mightily by God. So, I am just so thankful in spite of my flaws God has never held that against me. I am just a child of God that chose to serve Him.

Before receiving the Lord as my savior, I always wanted to be close to God. I didn't know before accepting His gift of salvation how to get it but I was always seeking. I would go to church across the street from my house, by myself as a child. When I got older, I would join a church but still didn't know how to be part of God's army. Even in my late teens I joined the women's missionary group, that had a meeting at someone's house every Monday night and I chose to be in the older ladies group instead of the one assigned for my age group and the older ladies would marvel at the fact that I wanted to be surrounded by them and not the younger ladies my age. I was not old fashioned or out of touch with my peers. I was right in step and in style with them but when it came to church I wanted to be surrounded by the older ladies. When I was witnessed to, I know what I was hearing was what I was looking for. All of 20 years of age and I had found the answer to my unasked questions. I know that I am not the only one that God has blessed with supernatural blessings, just one of many and I love Him for that. I found a lot of joy, in learning about Raphael. It started making changes in my life. I really didn't have that many concerns about that big warfare angel, he made his presence and purpose known just by his huge stature and how he was standing in my doorway. So, I didn't study much about him.

I believe the Lord has allowed my angels to almost show me who they are. Or from time to time allowed me to know that they are around me. One Sunday morning, at church some visitors came to service and there were children with them. I didn't pay attention to who came in with who, I was just aware that a family had just came in. If I am not in the pulpit I usually sit on the left side of the church up front. These children sat on the right-hand side of the pews towards the middle. After a few minutes I looked to my right at the children and there was a fair skinned girl about eight years old staring at me. Wow! She had the same face as my guardian angel, it was uncanny. But the strange thing was she never took her eyes off of me. I turned around and looked straight ahead. I waited a few minutes and looked again and there she was looking directly at me. It was so unreal I mean her face was exactly like my angel except her complexion was more olive than the whitish pink, but it was the same face.

Psalms 37:25 – David said, "I have been young and now am old, yet have I not seen the righteous forsaken nor his seed begging bread". And David knew what he was talking about. It's true, you won't ever see God's righteous, key word righteous, forsaken or overlooked nor his seed in need and begging bread. I am a living testimony of that scripture.

The main part of this visitation of my angels was to also introduce me to Raphael and the healing power he carries. Around the later part of September of the same year of 2003, on the 27th, I awoken with what I thought was the flu. I was in no pain, just a strong lack of energy. I did not feel like getting out of bed. This was on a Saturday, so I just rested. I believe I ate a little something, but I just wanted to lay around. I did get up and laid on the couch because that was all I wanted to do. I told my son I was not going to go to church I just wanted to stay home in bed. I went into a deep sleep and when I woke up on Sunday, I could smell something and saw that I had lost my bowels in my bed.

Wow! That was strange. I got up and took my sheets off the bed, put them in the washer, got clean sheets and took a shower. Doing all of that was like picking up a couch and carrying it over my head for two blocks. My energy was leaving. I put the sheets on my bed and went back to bed. I didn't tell my son because Moms just don't want to worry their children. I went back to bed and went back to sleep. I slept for a long time, in fact, I don't know how long and I don't remember eating at all. When I

awaken again, you guessed it, bowels lost again. This time I was extremely weak. I got up, took the sheets off, put them in the washer, but I was too weak to shower. I cleaned myself up, but also, I was too weak to put another set of sheets on the bed. So, I grabbed a couple of large bath towels and covered my mattress with them and went back to bed. Monday is a total blur and my son thought I was still battling the flu.

I made up my mind on Monday night that if things do not get better, I would go to the hospital. Tuesday came and there were no changes. I got up a 7 AM and I was ready at 10 AM. It took me three hours to pay my bills, because it was the end of the month, take a shower and get dressed. Something I could have done in one hour. My son was at school, so he knew nothing about my plans, and I had not told him what had occurred the days before. But I found out after I came home from the hospital, he had found out about the bowel thing. Let me pause here. Mothers are very protective over their children. Even though my sons were grown men, by this time, a mother knows their children and who can handle what. Of course, if I had been in pain or had a fever, I would have told them or someone to come see about me.

But we super Moms feel like, "I got this" or "I can handle this", they can't, not right now.

And about paying my bills, well since it was a day or so before the first of the month, I knew I had to handle my business. I have tried to make it a practice to be a wise steward, in handling my affairs. By the time I put the stamps on the envelopes I was exhausted. I opened my doors, got on the couch and dialed 911, The paramedics came, and they were the most wonderful group of people I had ever met.

They were very attentive and ever so caring. I explained what I was going through, and they said, "OK ma'am we are taking you to the hospital". I told them that I belonged to Kaiser and they told me to get on the gurney, but I could no longer move. All my strength was gone, but keep in mind, I am still in no pain.

When I got to emergency, they began to check my blood pressure and my blood. They asked me if I was a diabetic, and I told them no I was not. They kept checking and asked me again about being a diabetic and I told them no I was not. They told me the reason they keep asking because I had a sugar level of over 700 and they also let me know that they were getting my room ready. Before I was taken to my room, my son and two of his friends came in. I had left my son a note plus he said he knew something was wrong when he came in the house and I was not there, but my car was. What was so beautiful about my son's friends was they prayed for me, and that was such a blessing because it is wonderful to raise up your children in the way they should go. *Proverbs 22:6 - "Train up a child in the way he should go and when he is old, he will not depart from it".* And when you do this, they know what you have trained them to do and in, this case, pray, and that training filters over to the people they hang out with.

It was time for them to take me to my room, so my son and his friends left. As they began to wheel me to intensive care, I looked up and saw that I was in Room 333, and when I saw those three numbers I thought "Oh it's on now". I knew from that time I was going to be alright. Because God put me in that room to get the message to me that I was going to be alright.

The Number Three and What it means –Three stands for the solid, real, substantial, complete and entire.

All things that are especially complete are stamped with this number three.

God's attributes are three: Omniscience, Omnipresence and Omnipotence.

There are three great divisions completing time, past, present and future.

Three completes the sum of human capability, thought, word and deed.

As we have in the number one the sovereignty of the one God, and in the two the second person the Son, the great Deliverer. So, in three we have the third person The Holy Spirit, marking and completing the fulness of the Godhead. Three times the Seraphim cry "Holy, Holy, Holy, one for each of the three persons in the Trinity. ***Isaiah 6:3 and Revelation 4:8***

So, I had a working knowledge of the number three and all I really focused on was, three is the number of completions. I knew no matter what, I was going to be complete when I came out of the hospital. After I was settled, they told me my kidneys had stopped functioning and that my liver was on its way out. I didn't like what they were telling me, but I was in Room 333 and had already gotten my message from God. You got to trust and believe God. I called my cousin Barbara, my twin, (sadly she has gone home to be with the Lord). I knew she was the one to handle my business. We have kindred spirits and I knew she was the one to rely on. I loved her so. When my son finally came in my room after waiting for them to get me settled, I did what every child of God, that's in trouble, in need or sick should do. I took my cell phone and went from A to Z making a list of who my son is to call and let them know I was sick. And everyone on my list were those I knew would pray and get a prayer through.

Certain people were not on my list, simply because I knew they would come and look down on me and cry and believe I was going to die. On paper I was dying, my prognosis was poor and of course I loved them, but I meant business and I wanted to be covered and saturated with strong believers only. You see Raphael had already stepped into my life and I knew I was going to be healed. I was told after I got out of the hospital that the whites of my eyes were yellow. After they put in the catheter the nurses said that they had never seen urine that color before. I never got a chance to see it but others were talking about the strange color.

So, they told me what was going on in my body and then they told me I had to have a shunt put inside my body because I would need dialysis. At that moment I asked God, "is this how I am going to go out?" I didn't get angry about my situation; I was concerned but I certainly was not going to get mad with God and tell Him I got a bad deal. He knew what He was doing. I did not want to lose my integrity with God. After three days in intensive care, they told me I had to go to Oakland, which is a larger facility than Richmond and could better handle my situation. At least I was out of intensive care. They took me to Oakland

and put in the shunt which was a horrible experience. I am so glad I had praying people in my life because the first person who put in the shunt was not the right person to do it. There were several doctors with her, and I remember looking at her before she began. She closed her eyes real tight and began to tremble as if she was *psyching* herself out or putting herself in a trance before she started. I hated the whole ordeal, I just wanted them to make me dead, put in the shunt, then bring me back to life. It was as if I was the first living breathing person, she ever put a shunt in.

OK so now the shunt is in and the dialysis was to start the next day. Well later that night I put on my light so they could bring me some soap and water, so I could wash up. In ICU they bathed you but in the regular part of the hospital, they do not. Oh, I forgot to mention that I was paralyzed. I could only move my arms and my head. I had no control of the rest of my body. Whatever position I was stuck in, I was stuck. I could not turn over or use my legs to push myself up. But I could use my arms to wash myself while lying on my back, a shower was out of the question. So, they brought me some soap and water and they threw the covers back to assist me. When the nurse did, he gasped because I was laying there bleeding heavily from this misplaced shunt, the "tranced" doctor put in me. He said, "oh my God she is laying here bleeding to death". Now check this out, they could not find a doctor, nor contact one to come help me. So, they began to apply pressure, but every time they let up the blood would gush out. It amazes me how close a person could be to death and not know it. When I had my third child, I hemorrhaged so badly I almost died, so now here we go again. They finally put some weights in a sock and laid it on the gaping hole to stop the outpouring of blood. Thank God I wanted to wash, otherwise they would not have discovered that I was bleeding like a fat pig. I would have woken up the next day in Heaven, possibly.

So, you know what had to happen. Take this shunt out of me and put in another. Now keep in mind, this shunt was in my groin, Lord have mercy Jesus. After taking that one out they had to do it over and one of my doctors, who I could tell was very smart, was the one to do it and was the one I wanted in the first place. I did not ask him to do it, I mean, what do I know what he knows, but he was the one to do the procedure and this time it was in correctly. Now I got dialysis every other day or when necessary, plus insulin injections daily. And still the insulin was not bringing my sugar level down to a desired area. I had absolutely no appetite. I knew I had to eat, and I would try. I would put the food in my mouth but had no desire to swallow it. It was the weirdest thing and what I did taste was not bad, but all I had a desire to eat was the cold milk and the sugar free Jell-O. That's it, that's all

I would drink the Ensure because I knew I needed some nutrition in my body, and it was palatable but that kept me with runny uncontrollable bowels. In that experience I began to see how special nurses are. I would drink the Ensure, my bowels would take off and they would come and clean me up and change my bed and gown as if they just cleaned up an egg that cracked open on the floor. Nurses are not judgmental, they did not frown, they just did their job because they understand the sick. I gained more respect for them. Young, old, Black or White, American or other races, they all have the attitude of this person is sick, they cannot help themselves, they hate the position they are in. They are embarrassed and normally they are not like this and they need my help and understanding. I understand why they get paid as much as they do. When it comes to sickness and injuries, they have seen it all.

Nurses and doctors are special people.

So here I am, no appetite, paralyzed, no kidney function, shot with insulin all day, dialysis, liver failing, blood transfusion and arms dotted up from all the needles. But God. I had a lot to be thankful for I had caring family and praying people surrounding me every day. I had people laying hands on me, reading to me, calling on a regular basis, praying in my ear, surrounding my bed in circles praying for me, singing to me and friends visiting churches of people I knew telling them "your friend Sylvia is sick, in the hospital, go see her".

I am so blessed and was blessed by all my friends and family. One day my niece looked at me and said, "what are you doing here, get up. You don't look right laying here in the hospital". Wow! After about two weeks they came in and took the shunt out. Oh God, thank You Jesus! But when they took it out, I began to bleed profusely. The doctor, a cute one I may add, came in and began to apply pressure on this hole in my inner thigh that was bleeding like a volcano, but every time he would let up, the blood would gush out. He said, "I'm going to stand here and apply pressure until you stop bleeding, if it takes me all day." There's that extra mile again, or in my thinking, is this what true dedicated people in the medical field is made of? But I would not stop bleeding. Finally, he said in a stern voice, "do you believe in prayer?" and I said "yes". He then said, "well pray!". I began to pray and when he raised his hand up, I had stopped bleeding. Another doctor walked in and said, "has she stopped bleeding?" and the doctor said "yes, after I told her to pray." My doctor said that! You know during the whole ordeal of this, of course I prayed but I was not afraid and I didn't spend any time listening to Gospel songs or even reading the Word, in fact I didn't even have my Bible. I just trusted God with what I knew from experience. His Word is/was hidden in my heart.

I was just waiting for the day I would be released and back to normal. I was very aware that I had a whole army of prayer warriors, God believing people of faith praying for me and holding me up before

God, like Simba being raised up to the sky in, the movie, The Lion King. It was as if my prayer team was saying to God, "this is my friend Sylvia, she is sick, heal her, bring her back to us and her family 100% and even better. Bring her back so she can be a living testimony, that can share with others to help them believe in You". Removal of the shunt was good news. You know just before the shunt was removed and they were pushing me back to my room, in my bed, from having a dialysis treatment, a doctor was passing by and he stooped and looked over at me and said "Oh you will be alright, I have seen this before". "Seen what, I thought? Man, you didn't read my chart or asked questions, but you knew that I would be alright?" That incident had Divine written all over it. No shunt means no more dialysis, and also meaning my kidneys are functioning again and my liver was back to normal.

Shortly after that a doctor walked in and asked had I been sitting up in the past two weeks, and I said "no", and neither had I been to the bathroom own my own. I always had to use the bed pan. Someone came and got me out of my bed and let me sit up in a chair. That felt just wonderful. Sitting up in a chair is so underrated. A few days I was told that a nurse was going to take me to take a shower. Taking a shower is another underrated luxury. When I got in the shower and sat down and let the water run on my body, I thought I had died and went to heaven. The water was so refreshing and so soothing. OK so now

I got enough blood put back in me after the transfusions, three I believe and the shunt taken out of me, a chance to shower and sit up. Life is great! What's next? Time to walk or learn to walk again.

The physical therapist came with a walker and we began to walk down a long hall. He said, after the first time on the walker, "oh you will do just fine, just keep using the walker." I was so glad to be able to be upright and glad my legs could hold my weight and glad to be able to go to the bathroom on my own. The first time I went to the bathroom on my own with the walker was an experience. When I got to the bathroom and I looked in the mirror and I saw what others saw. I didn't like what I saw. I could tell by my face that I had been through a rough ordeal. I said to myself, "now I see why my family looked so worried". It was all in my face but that's not going to last long because I am on my way to recovery. The next night I went to the bathroom, I said "forget this walker". And I hobbled to the bathroom. The night nurse saw me and she said, in her most beautiful African accent, "Oh my God, look at you. You were so sick, now look at you". Yes, I hobbled and was bent over but I was on my two feet, on my own.

Other nurses the next day could not believe how well I was doing. They kept telling me how sick I was. I said, "I was?" I had no idea; I mean I really had no idea. Shortly after that I was told I would be going home soon. Thank God. The nurses showed me how to inject insulin and how to read the meter and shortly, I was released to go home. My son came and brought my clothes to put on and I noticed that they were way too big because in the three weeks, I had lost thirty-three pounds. There are those three's again. When I got in the car, and as my son drove off, he began to break down and cry. It all came out. He was so happy that I was better, and he was bringing me home.

I began to get stronger and stronger, but still unable to walk too far. I could drive places by myself but could not park too far away from where I was going. I did all I could independently to help regain my strength. One day after a doctor's appointment, I decided to visit my office to let them see I was on the road of recovery. When I walked in, after holding on to the walls, to get to my unit, they saw me, and their mouths flew open. I said, "close your mouths, yes it's me". They were glad to see me and gathered around me and they told me how well I looked and then they told me they thought I was going to die. One of my coworkers told me they were told, "go see Sly she doesn't look good and it looks bad". Little did they know I was so glad to see them and I would be returning to work shortly as soon as I am released by the doctors.

I knew I was sick, but I also knew I was not going to die. I knew it and God reassured me with that 333 on the first day going into intensive care. I knew I was going to come out solid, real, whole, complete and entire. When I was in the hospital, I did have some dreams of Heaven. God let me see this beautiful meadow with the grass a color of green I have never seen before and is not easy to describe, you had to be there. When the wind blew the grass moved like water. It was tall and beautiful and a grass you would not want to cut, because when you walked through it, it would open and gave you a path to walk through. He also showed me a small beautiful dog that was a shade of blue, the human eye has never beheld and when you stroked it, it's fur would turn a bluish, green, and lavender like never ever seen before. I can say I have had a peek. Just a peek. I can only imagine what Heaven is like.

When I returned to work, I still had to hold onto the walls as I walked and I was still under the doctor's care, even though I was released to return to work. And I was happy to return to work because I was focused on regaining my strength. My supervisor was glad I was back because I am a fast worker, so I was able to clear out a lot of work that had piled up and was too much work for the other clerk. Our office was the only two clerk unit, when all the other units had just one clerk. Plus, I did enjoy my job. Let me say this, even though this was my second time working a long term job I enjoyed this job because in my job before this, there were times I had very difficult assignments that I didn't enjoy because that was a highly technical company. But this position, even though there was a lot of work, was easier to understand which made the position enjoyable even though there was a whole lot more work to do. I often gave praises to God for doing it that way because He made my final years of working extremely easy. God always know what is best for us.

Even though I was back at work, I still wasn't at 100 percent. They told me I could come back part time and work my way back to full time. But I insisted on full time. I wanted to regain my strength as quickly as I could. Now here's where favor, on my job kicked in. My supervisor brought a petition and had the janitors bring down a cot and she made a little "nook", by the wall so I could go and rest and sleep for as long as I needed, about an hour, along with taking my lunch, and taking my breaks and she never said one word. She could have said, "you know what Sly, you are sleeping too long, you are still weak, you need to go to part time". But she never did, and she let me take all the rest I needed until I began to get stronger. There is no way the other company I worked for would do this.

On the first Sunday, I was able to go to church, and as soon as I walked in everyone started to praise God. I threw my purse and my Bible in the pews and praised God with them. They had seen me in the hospital, and they knew what I had been through. Plus, I made it a point to visit every church of my friends to let them see God's miracle. Plus, I love surprising people. One church I went to the pastor who is also a good friend, he and his wife, looked up and said "What?" He said, "Where is your wheelchair, where is your cane and where is your walker?" I said, "I don't know because I don't own any of those things".

Although I was back to work, I was still injecting myself with insulin, which I hated. So, one day my doctor called and said she was going to put me on a pill. So, I was happy about that. When I got the prescription filled, it said on the bottle "for the non-insulin dependent", so I took that to mean that I should take no more insulin. I stopped injecting insulin and was taking the pills as prescribed. Now I noticed I started getting that jittery feeling because my sugar was low and I kept soda and candy at my desk for that sugar rush I needed. After about two weeks my doctor called and asked me how I was doing. I told her that the pills were keeping my sugar level low, but I get jittery at times.

She also asked me how much insulin I was taking, and I said, I was taking none. She said "none?", You are supposed to take insulin with the pills. I told her what it said on the bottle and I took that to mean so insulin. Then she said she was confused and would call me back the next day which would have been on a Thursday. I decided to not take the pill nor the insulin because since she was confused, I made sure I wasn't.

A couple of days went by and she still had not called. She finally called on that Saturday afternoon and she asked me how much insulin I was giving myself. I said none. She then asked my how many pills I was taking, and I also said none. Then she asked me what my sugar count and I had told her it was normal. Then she said, "well I guess you're not a diabetic", and I was like, "I guess I'm not".

God healed me, fixed me and is my Doctor. Divine is all I can say. Hopefully, she is a better doctor than she was then, I won't put her down. I believe in doctors and nurses and care givers, but there are times God steps in and get your case over with so you can get on with your life and His plans for you. My Angels made themselves known early in the year for what was to come, so I can be prepared. I am glad I know I have them and that they made themselves known and you have them too! I am no different than you and God is not a respecter of persons. What He does for one He does for others and I am so grateful.

Now remember earlier, I said during my angel visitation, my grandson was with me. I asked God what the reason was, that he was present, and He said because my grandson have those same three angels, as well. The Guardian Messenger Angel, Raphael the Angel of Healing, Travel and Good Marriages and the Warring Angel that protects me, All three. And guess what? My grandson's middle name is Rafael.

Bless God and thank You Lord for being so generous. So full of selfless abundance. I love You Dear Lord.

The testimonies in this book is just a drop in the ocean. Just one raindrop, just one leaf off a tree, of all He has done for me. This is my heart share to you, to aid you in believing the awesome things God has in store for you. The many ways He can and will bless you, just believe, you have just gone on a short journey with me and my life in Christ. Yes, there have been, heartbreaks, heartaches, disappointments, let downs, rejections, put on the back shelf and the back burner, pain, losses, moments of fear and many days and nights of tears, but I have never felt alone or forgotten by God, never. And I love Him for that because He says He will never leave us or forsake us, and He has kept His every word.

I hope this book has been a blessing to you and will help you believe, trust and keep your hand in God's hand and hold on to His Everlasting arm. The Lord of Lords, the Prince of Peace the Lover of our souls.

And remember the testimonies of the great and wonderful things God has done for us have no shelf life. Your testimonies, no matter how long ago that it happened is still as fresh as the day it happened. Your testimony brings life at the time you share it. When your testimony is needed, the Holy Spirit will bring it back to your memory to share, at the time. Even if the testimony is not fresh in your mind all the time, when you share it, it becomes brand new again. The joy of having such testimonies to share will bring a load of fresh tears, a deluge of goosebumps and a whole day of praises, all over again.

Daily Prayer To Start Your Day

I am leaving you with a prayer that The Lord gave me in 1999, to repeat daily. This prayer covers your day when you say it early in the morning,

Here is a prayer the Lord blessed me with, to write in 1999. It is a prayer that covers just about whatever may happen for that day. It is to be read every morning and it will bless you. After repeating this prayer, you will begin to memorize it and it will become a part of your life. I do hope and pray that it becomes a part of your everyday practice. This prayer was written from my heart with you in mind.

"I thank You Lord for keeping me through the night and keeping my family and Lord I thank You for being on my mind, even in my sleep. Lord today whatever Your will is for my life, let everything be carried out. Let my decisions and actions be the ones that You will get the most Glory from. God make sure that every morsel of food that I put into my body today is blessed and is for the nourishment of my body.

If You choose to use me today, let me hear Your voice in my spirit so I will know what it is that You want me to do. If what You want me to do involves other people, let them only see You and not the incomplete, imperfect vessel. Lord go before me in every area and every place that I go. Place Your Grace and Mercy on each side of me, behind me and most of all before me.

Thank You for being with me, this day. I ask everything in Jesus' Precious Name.

Your Humble Servant...Amen.

www.ingramcontent.com/pod-product-compliance
Lightning Source LLC
Chambersburg PA
CBHW071227090426

42736CB00014B/2996